Tourism in Japan

TOURISM AND CULTURAL CHANGE
Series Editors: Mike Robinson, *Centre for Tourism and Cultural Change, Leeds Metropolitan University, Leeds, UK* and Alison Phipps, *University of Glasgow, Scotland, UK*

Understanding tourism's relationships with culture(s) and vice versa is of ever-increasing significance in a globalizing world. This series will critically examine the dynamic inter-relationships between tourism and culture(s). Theoretical explorations, research-informed analyses and detailed historical reviews from a variety of disciplinary perspectives are invited to consider such relationships.

Full details of all the books in this series and of all our other publications can be found on http://www.channelviewpublications.com, or by writing to Channel View Publications, St Nicholas House, 31-34 High Street, Bristol, BS1 2AW, UK.

TOURISM AND CULTURAL CHANGE
Series Editors: Mike Robinson and Alison Phipps

Tourism in Japan
An Ethno-Semiotic Analysis

Arthur Asa Berger

CHANNEL VIEW PUBLICATIONS
Bristol • Buffalo • Toronto

Library of Congress Cataloging in Publication Data
A catalog record for this book is available from the Library of Congress.
Berger, Arthur Asa, 1933-
Tourism in Japan: An Ethno-Semiotic Analysis/Arthur Asa Berger.
Includes bibliographical references and index.
1. Tourism--Japan. 2. Tourism--Social aspects--Japan. I. Title.
G155.J27B47 2010
306.4'8190952–dc22 2009052526

British Library Cataloguing in Publication Data
A catalogue entry for this book is available from the British Library.

ISBN-13: 978-1-84541-134-3 (hbk)
ISBN-13: 978-1-84541-133-6 (pbk)

Channel View Publications
UK: St Nicholas House, 31-34 High Street, Bristol, BS1 2AW, UK.
USA: UTP, 2250 Military Road, Tonawanda, NY 14150, USA.
Canada: UTP, 5201 Dufferin Street, North York, Ontario, M3H 5T8, Canada.

The policy of Multilingual Matters/Channel View Publications is to use papers that are natural, renewable and recyclable products, made from wood grown in sustainable forests. In the manufacturing process of our books, and to further support our policy, preference is given to printers that have FSC and PEFC Chain of Custody certification. The FSC and/or PEFC logos will appear on those books where full certification has been granted to the printer concerned.

Typeset by Techset Composition Ltd., Salisbury, UK.
Printed and bound in Great Britain by Short Run Press Ltd.

Dedication

This book is dedicated to the memory of three of my favourite professors at the University of Massachusetts in Amherst, where I studied between 1950 and 1954: Ian MacIver, Ray Ethan Torrey and Maxwell Henry Goldberg.

Contents

Acknowledgements xi

Foreword xiii

Preface xvii

Part 1: Japan as a Tourist Destination 1

1   Japan as a Tourist Destination: An Analytic Perspective 3
    Statistics about Japan 3
    Statistics on Japanese Family Income and Expenditures 5
    Defining Tourism 5
    Popular Kinds of Tourism in Japan 7
    The Imagined Japan, the 'Real' Japan and the
        Remembered Japan 10
    Guidebook Perspectives on Japan 13
    Japanese National Character 17
    John Gunther and Stereotypes of the Japanese 21
    Some Tours of Japan 24
    A Suggested Itinerary of Japan 26
    The Japan National Tourist Organization's Japan 28
    Uses and Gratifications of Tourism in Japan 29
    Conclusions 32

2   Japan and the Tourism Industry 35
    Statistics on World Tourism 35
    What Americans Do When They Visit Japan 40
    Activities of Japanese Tourists in Foreign Countries 41
    Japanese Tourists in Bali 42
    Conclusions 43

3   Japan on the Internet 45
    Googling Japan 45
    'Japan Tourism' on Google 47
    Japan on YouTube 48
    Conclusions 48

Part 2: Semiotic Japan 51

4   Semiotic Japan 53
    Introduction 53
    A Brief Note on Semiotic Theory 53
    Codes 56
    Sumo Wrestlers 57
    Geishas 61
    The Geisha and the Salaryman 68
    The Japanese Flag 69
    School Uniforms and Hikikomori: Japan's Hermit Youth 71
    Japanese Baseball 77
    Rock Gardens (kare sansui) 79
    Sanja Matsuri Festival in Asakusa 81
    Manga (Japanese Comic Books) 85
    High-Tech Toilets 93
    Vending Machines 96
    7-Eleven Convenience Stores 98
    Pachinko 99
    Gift Giving in Japan 103
    100 Yen Stores 108
    Department Stores (Hyakkaten or Departōs) 109
    The Tokyo Subway Map 112
    Fugu and Blue-finned Tuna: Fish Madness in Japan 115
    Bento Boxes 117
    Conclusions on Japanese Icons and Daily Life 118

5   Tourism and Cultural Change in Japan 121
    Classical Theories of Social Change 122
    Kinds of Tourists and Cultural Change 124
    Sources of Cultural Change 125
    Tourism's Cultural Impact on Japan 129
    The Place of this Book in the Cultural Tourism Series 130

6   Coda: A Return to Japan 132
    Our First Encounters with Helpful Japanese Persons 132
    The Sanja Matsuri Festival in Asakusa 133
    Lost in the Shimbashi Subway Station 135
    Expect To Be Lost Many Times in Japan 135
    Travelling by Long-Distance Buses in Japan 136
    Takayama Adventures 137
    Kanazawa 139

Last Day in Kanazawa 140
More on Food Courts in Department Stores 140
An Aside on Japanese Supermarkets 142
On to Kyoto 142
Teaching Japanese Students about American Humour 144
Visits to Himeji and Nara 147
The United States and Japan: A Study in Polarities 150

References 152
Index 155

Acknowledgements

I would like to thank Yasutake Tsukamoto and his colleagues at the Japan National Tourist Organization for supplying me with data and other information that I have used in this book. I also owe an enormous debt of gratitude to Naomi Chiba, a Japanese sociologist, who was my main informant on Japanese society and its popular culture. Her help has been invaluable.

I obtained a great deal of useful information about Japan from more than a dozen books I consulted, each offering somewhat different suggestions about places to go to and things that tourists visiting Japan can do. I also read a number of what might be called 'a year in Japan travel memoirs' such as Bruce S. Feiler's *Learning to Bow: Inside the Heart of Japan*, Gary Katzenstein's *Funny Business: An Outsider's Year in Japan* and Cathy N. Davidson's *36 Views of Mount Fuji*. I read Alex Kerr's highly critical study, *Lost Japan*, and a journal by Donald Richie, *The Japanese Journals 1947–2004*, which covered almost 60 years of his writings, meetings and matings with people in the arts (and many others as well) in Japan. These books provided me with personal experiences the authors had and insights they could offer about their time in Japan, and helped me gain a more complex picture of Japanese culture and society.

I found much interesting material in Edwin O. Reischauer and Marius B. Jansen's *The Japanese Today: Change and Continuity* and Edward Seidensticker's *Tokyo Rising: The City Since the Great Earthquake*. I also found Patrick Smith's critique of Reischauer's work, *Japan: A Reinterpretation*, often to be quite compelling and Takie Sugiyama Lebra and William P. Lebra's (1986) edited volume, *Japanese Culture and Behavior: Selected Readings (Revised Edition)*, to have a number of useful articles in it. I have used quotations from various books and articles on Japan at the beginning of chapters and in various places in my chapters when they are relevant. They provide fascinating insights into Japanese society. Japan has developed a unique, distinctive and prodigiously complex and difficult to understand culture. These quotations help us gain perspectives on Japan that are very useful.

I also want to thank Professor Sachiko Kitazume and Professor Goh Abe for arranging a lecture on humour at Kinki University in Osaka and for working valiantly to translate some of the ideas I dealt with in my lecture to the students to whom I lectured. My lecture was on visual humour and it was quite a challenge to explain the humour in *Peanuts*, *Krazy Kat* and other comic strips and cartoons to Japanese students. I am very grateful to Professor Abe for writing the Foreword to this book. I also want to thank Mariko Watanabe for allowing me to use a selection from an e-mail message she sent to people who took tours with her in Japan. A friend of mine who toured with her sent me her e-mail. A special word of thanks to Lucy Corne for letting me use her splendid photograph of a sumo wrestling match.

I am grateful to the editors of this series, Michael D. Robinson and Alison Phipps, for accepting my book for their series on tourism and cultural change, and to Sarah Williams, my editor at Channel View Publications, for her efforts on my behalf. Cultural change is, you will see, the subtext of this book.

Finally, I would like to thank the people of Japan, who received us so graciously, and the many others who helped us on the numerous occasions when we were lost and trying to find our way to some subway or train station, temple, department store or other destination in various cities of Japan. We never needed help in finding any 7-Eleven stores because they are everywhere.

Foreword

Arthur Asa Berger's book *Tourism in Japan: An Ethno-Semiotic Analysis*, one of a series of books published by Channel View Publications on tourism and cultural change around the world, reflects his ethno-semiotic approach to the subject. He collected his data as both a traveller and a fieldworker. For Berger, 'cultures are composed of a wide variety of codes or ways of behaving, rules that are passed on from generation to generation that affect human relationships. They are directives, often quite specific, that often function below our levels of awareness'.

His objects of analysis are aspects of Japanese cultures that tourists frequently encounter such as the Japanese flag, Japanese school children in their uniforms, Japanese baseball, Zen rock gardens, geishas, the Sanja Matsuri festival in Asakusa, department stores, manga, the Tokyo subway system map and sumo wrestlers. Berger aptly points out that underneath these cultural elements, in the case of school children who become hermits (the Hikikomori), are 'enormous unresolved social and cultural problems in Japan'. We Japanese have not yet found the solutions to this problem and others like it.

If I were asked to write a book on American culture and tourism, I would have focused on what I have observed in the United States since my first initiation into the American culture in 1969 as a foreign student. I remained there for more than eight years as a graduate student. I would have written about American baseball, American football, the west, the NY subway, various kinds of ethnic festivals, department stores in big cities and guns. For Americans, these phenomena are things they tend to take for granted; the average American does not believe they have any social or cultural significance at all. Japanese tourists in America might find them interesting but, generally speaking, would not recognize their cultural significance.

One example of interest involves his discussion of high-tech toilets. His analysis of the hidden meanings of these toilets suggests that they reflect, among other things, Japanese perfectionism and attitudes towards bodily waste. He also deals with topics such as the ubiquitous 7-Eleven convenience stores, along with *Pachinko* (an amusement particularly well suited to the Japanese temperament), gift giving and 100 yen stores. As a Japanese person, I am quite sure that 100 yen stores seem very strange to many tourists from overseas. We Japanese welcome such stores as a place where we can buy a variety of daily goods for about a dollar.

Berger continually asks his readers to consider the hidden meanings of the topics he discusses. As he writes, 'I have offered, in my analysis, insights into the hidden significance of any number of different icons of Japanese everyday life and culture that I believe will enrich and enhance the insights tourists gain from their visits to Japan'. In his chapter 'Tourism and Culture Change', he points out that a subtext of his book is the way in which Japanese society and culture have evolved over the years, suggesting that tourists are 'agents of social and cultural change'. I quite agree with this point of view and believe that tourists have been agents of cultural change in Japan, although we Japanese may not always recognize the dimensions of these changes and how these changes have come about.

At the end of the book, he offers a personal narrative of his journeys in Japan. We Japanese can read this chapter as his attempt, as a tourist, to find a way of adapting to, as well as interpreting, Japanese society and culture. The chapter can be used as an example of how to record differences and similarities between Japan and the United States and changes that have taken place in Japanese society and culture in recent decades. In Japan, Berger's book might very well be used as a text for Japanese high school and college students who are interested not only in the cultural differences but also in the similarities between Japan and the United States.

Goh Abe

Old Japan is dead and gone, and Young Japan reigns in its stead . . . .The steam-whistle, the newspaper, the voting-paper, the pillar-post at every street corner and even in remote villages, the clerk shop or bank or public office hastily summoned from our side to answer the ring of the telephone bell replacing the palanquin, the iron-clad replacing the war-junk, – these and a thousand other startling changes testify that Japan is transported ten thousand miles away from her former moorings . . . Nevertheless . . . it is abundantly clear to those who have dived beneath the surface of the modern Japanese upheaval that more of the past has been retained than has been let go . . . It is that the national character persists intact, manufacturing no change in essentials. Circumstances have deflected it into new channels, that is all. (Chamberlain, 1905/2007)

The natural beauty of Tohoku (Tohoku is a northern area of Japan) was enchanting, but the towns and villages proved a little disappointing. I could not help recognizing that the old Japan I have long sought has been rapidly disappearing. Westernization and urbanization are taking its toll on the life-style of even the most remote locations in Japan. (Mariko Watanabe, e-mail message)

Preface

Japan is a country with countless attractions of interest – a remarkable traditional culture that still exists, and an exciting and vibrant popular culture. The Japanese people tend to be xenophobic and many of them divide the world into two parts: people and things Japanese and everything and everyone else. So while individual Japanese people may be extraordinarily friendly and helpful to tourists, I have been told by Americans who have lived in Japan that the Japanese really do not welcome people from foreign lands living there because of a Japanese obsession with racial purity.

It is also a very safe country to visit, with a very low crime rate. But because it *can* be quite expensive, it does not have large numbers of foreign tourists visiting it relative to many other countries. Around 75 million tourists visit France every year while around 8 million tourists visit Japan. The image of Japan as a terribly expensive country has prevented many people who would find Japan a wonderful place to visit from going there. Tours to Japan often cost twice as much as tours to countries such as Thailand or Vietnam. In Thailand and Vietnam I stayed at perfectly decent hotels for $25, including breakfast, while the least expensive hotel I could find in Japan was around $80. And transportation in Japan is expensive, even if you take long-distance buses instead of bullet trains.

However, if you travel on your own and stay in business hotels, such as those found in the Toyoko Inn chain (which cost around 8000 yen or about $80 for a double room), take advantage of set price meals in restaurants at lunch time, and avoid going to very expensive restaurants, you can visit Japan for little more than you would spend in many other countries and much less than in many European countries now that the dollar is so weak and the euro is so strong. Tokyo is now a bargain for Americans when compared to a city like London and Japan is not more expensive than many European countries any more.

There are around 200 Toyoko Inns in Japan and many other cheap hotels, Ryokans and other kinds of lodging for travellers. [The Toyoko Inn website is www.toyoko-inn.com/eng/ and you can find a list of all the Toyoko Inns there.] Japan also has an enormous number of cheap dining options – everything from noodle shops and the ubiquitous

7-Eleven stores and other convenience stores that sell Bento lunch boxes and other kinds of prepared food to fast-food places and modestly priced restaurants in department stores – so you need not spend a fortune to eat well in Japan. Many Japanese restaurants have set-price lunches at noon that cost between $8 and $10 (and sometimes a few dollars more) for a complete meal. And there's no tipping in Japanese restaurants, either.

Tourism and Ethno-Semiotic Analysis

This book is a study of Japanese tourism and an ethnographic investigation (i.e. one based on personal observation and analysis) of iconic aspects of contemporary Japanese culture and society. I developed this approach to studying tourism in various cultures after reading Roland Barthes' brilliant study of Japan, *Empire of Signs*, which deals with such things as *Pachinko*, Japanese chopsticks, bowing, railway stations, the 'empty' centre of Tokyo and tempura. Barthes cautions his readers that he is not 'photographing' Japan, by which he means offering a systematic and all-encompassing study of the country, but, instead, 'flashes', studies of specific topics that caught his eye. What struck Barthes was that in Japan he found 'an unheard-of symbolic system, one altogether detached from our own' (Barthes, 1982: 3). My analysis will also involve 'flashes' that involve important Japanese icons, objects, fads, fashions and rituals and will not attempt to offer a more comprehensive or systematic study of Japanese society and culture, although I do say a good deal about the Japanese education system and other aspects of Japanese culture.

Japan is a curious combination of hyper-modernism and postmodernism in its huge cities like Tokyo, and ancient traditions, seen in its temples, shrines, religious festivals, ancient costumes and many other aspects of Japanese traditional culture. Basil Hall Chamberlain, who was a professor of Japanese at the University of Tokyo, wrote his book *Things Japanese* more than 100 years ago. He suggested that although Japan was modernizing, the essential Japanese character had not changed. Whether he would agree with his original assessment now, that the various aspects of contemporary Japan that seem so strange to foreign tourists are only superficial, is difficult to know. His book, written, as he puts it, 'for travellers and others', has an alphabetical format and discusses everything from the abacus (his first topic) to zoology (his last topic). His goal, of digging beneath the surface and explaining the hidden significance of objects, rituals and practices, is one that I attempt in this book.

When tourists visit countries, they generally go in search of activities that will enable them to have interesting and pleasant experiences. They hope their visits will enable them to understand people better and to see their own lives and lifestyles more clearly. It is through differences that we learn the meaning of things, and most tourists find Japan very different from any other country they have ever visited. Japan is a fascinating country, with a refined aesthetic that permeates many aspects of Japanese daily life and culture. I believe it is this aesthetic that mesmerizes so many foreign tourists, who spend their time viewing Japan's cultural treasures and avoid parts of everyday life in Japan that they do not find very attractive. Tourism is an extremely segmented industry, and tourists are quite selective about what they want to do and see when they visit a foreign country like Japan.

In the first part of the book, I will examine the tourism industry in Japan and discuss matters such as where tourists to Japan come from, how Japan rates as a tourism destination, and where Japanese tourists go and what they do when they travel abroad. This section will be based on information I have obtained from the internet, the Japanese National Tourist Organization (JNTO) and a number of other sources.

The second part of the book is devoted to an applied semiotic analysis of Japanese culture and society, primarily as experienced by tourists. When Barthes described Japan as an 'empire of signs', he called our attention to the important objects and rituals (in semiotic theory they are called signifiers) that offered insights into Japanese culture and society. Semiotics is the study of signs, which can be defined as anything that stands for something else, anything that conveys meaning. How signs convey meaning is what semiotics deals with, and semiotic theory can be quite arcane and very technical. I will discuss a few basic concepts in semiotics that will help you understand what I am doing in more detail shortly.

Ethnography is a social science research method in which observation plays an important role. That is, the experiences of the investigator are important. Many anthropological studies are ethnographic in nature. As Claude Lévi-Strauss, one of the greatest anthropologists of recent years, writes in his work *Tristes Tropiques*:

> It may seem strange that I should so long have remained deaf to a message which had after all been transmitted for me ever since I first began to read philosophy, by the masters of the French school of sociology. The revelation did not come to me, as a matter of fact, till 1933 or 1934 when I came upon a book which was already by no means new: Robert H. Lowie's *Primitive Society*. But instead of notions borrowed from books and at once metamorphosed into philosophical concepts I was confronted by an account of first-hand experience. The observer, moreover, had been so committed as to keep intact the full meaning of his experience. (Lévi-Strauss, 1970: 62–63)

What Lévi-Strauss is suggesting is that 'first-hand' experience by careful observers can yield important insights into cultures.

The difference between a casual tourist and a social scientist using participant observation is that travellers and tourists are interested in being informed and entertained and in having interesting and life-enriching experiences, but they do not, as a rule, probe the social and cultural significance of their experiences the way social scientists do. And they are not as careful in their observations as social scientists are. Semiotics is an interpretative form of social science and thus one must always question the validity of the interpretations semioticians offer. But that is the nature of all the social sciences. In the final analysis, there is always an element of interpretation of data – even in economics, the most mathematical of the social sciences.

This book is based on my experiences in Japan during two visits there, and is also based on information about Japanese culture and tourism that I found in books, in magazine and newspaper articles, on the internet and from informants – Japanese sociologists and scholars who offered me information about subjects that interested me. I also benefited greatly from reading a number of travel memoirs and other books about Japan, mentioned in my acknowledgements section. All these books dealt with the experiences the writers had in Japan and offered valuable insights into Japanese culture and society.

While my book is a scholarly study of tourism in Japan and of Japanese culture, I have written it in an accessible style, one that is easy to follow; hence it will also be of interest to tourists who plan to visit Japan and are interested in gaining insights into certain aspects of Japanese traditional culture, popular culture and everyday life that conventional guidebooks about Japan generally do not provide in any depth. I make considerable use of quotations so that my readers can see the actual language used by the various experts and commentators I have consulted.

In the first paragraph of the first chapter of Barthes' *Empire of Signs*, titled 'Faraway', he writes:

> If I want to imagine a fictive nation, I can give it an invented name, treat it declaratively as a novelistic object, create a new Garabagne, so as to compromise no real country by my fantasy (though in no way claiming to represent or to analyze reality itself (these being the major gestures of Western discourse) – islolate somewhere in the world (*faraway*) a certain number of features (a term employed in linguistics), and out of these features deliberatively form a system. It is the system which I shall call: Japan.

That, in a sense, is what I will be doing, and my focus will be as eclectic as Barthes' was. I will be interpreting the meaning of the signs that tourists generally experience in Japan – in some cases covering topics he did, but in other cases dealing with phenomena in which he was not interested. I will interpret, analyse and explicate various aspects of Japanese everyday life, culture and society that most people encounter when they travel there.

On the personal level, I became fascinated with Japan in 1951 when I saw Kurosawa's *Rashomon*. This film is credited with making film lovers aware of the existence and greatness of Japanese films. It is a film that is still with me and has shaped my thinking over the years. When I taught media criticism, I used to show it at the beginning of my courses. I see *Rashomon* as a postmodern film, one in which it is impossible to know what happened in a grove between a bandit, a samurai and the samurai's wife. The events in the grove were also witnessed by a woodcutter. What makes the film so remarkable, aside from the brilliant cinematography and wonderful acting, was that each of the four main characters in the film had a completely different version of what went on in that grove.

Tourism and Cultural Change in Japan

The title of this book, *Tourism in Japan*, suggests its focus – namely a study of Japanese culture and the tourism industry. And the subtitle, *An Ethno-Semiotic Analysis*, suggests my focus – on how semiotics can be used to interpret Japanese culture. My book is also relevant to the title of this series, 'Tourism and Cultural Change'. It is instructive to look at two extreme iconic examples of Japanese culture. There is a world of difference between the quiet and serene Zen rock gardens tourists visit in Japan, icons of the old Japan, and the screamingly loud *Pachinko* parlours tourists pass, and sometimes – out of curiosity – drop in on in the course of their trips, powerful icons of the new Japan.

I have imagined prototypical tourists visiting Japan and analysed many of the things these tourists might do and see, such as visiting temples and Zen rock gardens, attending a sumo wrestling match, seeing school children in their uniforms and sampling Japanese food. Tourism is now the largest industry in the world. As such, it is reasonable to suggest that tourism plays an important role in generating social and cultural change. Tourists all over the world are spreading their beliefs, assumptions and expectations and bringing their financial resources to each other's countries. The countries that tourists visit generally do what they can to attract as many tourists as possible and to offer them the kind of experiences they seek.

In his influential book, *The Tourist: A New Theory of the Leisure Class*, Dean MacCannell (1976: 23) writes that 'all tourist attractions are cultural experiences'. He adds that cultural experiences have two parts: the first he calls 'representation' and the second 'influence', since 'all cultures are a series of models of life'. It is reasonable to assume that the models of culture that tourists bring to foreign countries influence the way in which these countries respond to tourists, whether it involves building new roads and transportation networks, and new hotels, or supporting distinctive cultural institutions. Tourists are, then, agents of social and cultural change. I hope that readers of this book will find, among other things, that it offers insights into Japanese culture and society and deals with some of the changes that have taken place there that are shaping contemporary Japanese culture and society.

Note

1. All the photographs in this book were taken by me. All the charts and figures are my constructions and based on information from various sources.

Part 1

Japan as a Tourist Destination

Japan? That was where my grandparents came from, it didn't have much to do with my present life ... For me Japan was cheap baseballs, Godzilla, weird sci-fi movies like Star Man, *where you could see the strings that pulled him above his enemies, flying in front of a backdrop so poorly made even I, at eight, was conscious of the fakery ... Of course, by the eighties, I was aware, as everyone else was, of Japan's burgeoning power, its changing image – Toyota, Nissan, Toshiba, the economic, electronic, automotive miracle. Rather than savage barbarism the Japanese now were characterized by a frightening efficiency and a tireless energy. Japan was a monster of industrialization, of huge, world-hungry corporations. Unfair trade practices, the trade imbalance. Robot people.* (David Mura, 1991)

In Japan, one felt as if the world had been turned upside down and inside out, all its values and assumptions turned on their heads – as if, one might say, the force of gravity had been so radically altered that one had ended up on another planet. It sometimes seemed – and Japan liked to make it seem – as if Japan had a different epicenter from the rest of the world, as if, indeed, all the rest of the world inhabited a Copernican, and Japan, a Ptolemaic, universe; and so, where much of the rest of the world traditionally looked to America as its center, Japan looked only to Japan. America might be a fashion accessory, a collectible, a sign of imported glamour; but it was not the end-point of most aspirations here. America was an alternative to Gucci, not to Bushido *or Emperor worship or Japan.* (Pico Iyer, 1991)

1

Japan as a Tourist Destination: An Analytic Perspective

Japan is a chain of more than 3000 islands that stretches for more than 1800 miles, from close to Siberia in the north to almost reaching Taiwan in the south. The four largest islands, where most of the population is to be found, are Hokkaido, Honshu, Shikoku and Kyushu. There are 46 prefectures in Japan. It is a constitutional monarchy with an emperor who is seen as a divine figure by many Japanese people. For most tourists, Japan is a very enigmatic country, for reasons that will become evident as you read this book. Let me start by offering some statistics about Japan that will provide some insights into why Japanese culture and society developed the way they did.

Statistics about Japan

Statistics about Japan are quite extraordinary. Japan has Tokyo, the largest city in the world with 35 million people living in the greater Tokyo conurbation. Japan has half the industrial robots in the world. It leads the world in life expectancy and, yet, it also leads the developed nations in the number of suicides committed every year. Japanese high school students rate very highly on tests of mathematical knowledge and reading skills, but the Japanese educational system, with its focus on rote memory and its problem with bullying, is considered by many education scholars a disaster area. The statistics that follow offer some insights into the strengths of Japanese society and some of the problems that Japan faces. The data come from a variety of sources such as the CIA fact book for Japan, Wikipedia, and various books, newspaper and magazine articles:

- 128 million people. Tenth largest country in terms of population.
- 43% of the American population in 4% of the space.

- More than 50% of Japanese women are single at 30 (37% in USA).
- 29.6% of the population are over 65 (19.2% in USA).
- The 1.34 birth rate is below replacement levels (2.08 in USA).
- In 2015 one in four persons in Japan will be elderly.
- Literacy rate: 99%.
- Average monthly household income (2008): 476,000 yen (around $4760).
- Average monthly household expenditures (2008): 275,000 yen (around $2750).
- More than 80% own cameras.
- One million hikikomori – young recluses withdrawn from society.
- 15,000 7-Eleven stores in Japan (1500 in Tokyo).
- Tokyo downtown: 8 million people.
- Greater Tokyo Area: 35 million people (largest in the world).
- 377,835 km^2 (152,000 square miles, almost the size of California).
- Population density: 836 per square mile (California: 217 per square mile).
- Ethnicity: 99% Japanese; 1% other ethnicities.
- 11.64% of the country is arable land.
- Very low birth rate. Population estimated to shrink to 100 million by 2050.
- Highest life expectancy in the world: 81.25 years.
- 30,000 suicides per year since 1998 (24 per 100,000; USA: 11 per 100,000).
- 10,000 deaths per year due to overwork.
- 273 billion cigarettes sold in 2006 (USA: 370 billion).
- Second largest economy in the world (4.5 trillion dollar GNP).
- 50% of the world's industrial robots are in Japan.
- Third in the world on the amount of money spent on research and development.
- Shinto religion is dominant; Buddhism and Confucianism are important.
- Kyoto is the cultural centre. 1.4 million people.
- 38% of all books sold in Japan are manga (comics).
- Important cell phone culture with much text messaging.
- An important source of video games, animated films and other popular culture.
- Not in the top 20 foreign tourism countries.
- Fifteen-year-olds: sixth best in the world in Japanese knowledge and skills.

Statistics on Japanese Family Income and Expenditures

In 2008, according to the Japanese Statistics Bureau, the average monthly family income in Japan was roughly 400,000 yen a month, which at 100 yen to the dollar comes out to 4000 a month or approximately USD 48,000 a year, not including yearly bonuses, which are often quite large. With a bonus, the average family income rises to around $60,000 a year. In the United States, the average family income is also around $60,000 a year. The disposable income in the average Japanese family is 300,000 yen or USD 30,000 a year. In two-or-more-person households, the expenditures per month are (all figures rounded out and calculated at 100 yen to the dollar) given in Table 1.1.

These figures do not show how much income Japanese people pay for their travel and whether their travel expenses come out of culture and recreation expenses or their other consumption expenditures. But as Table 2.5 shows, Japan ranks fourth in the world in per capita tourism expenses.

Defining Tourism

Tourism scholars are not in agreement about how to define the term 'tourist', and there are a number of different definitions of the term. Some say that any kind of travel, even for business purposes, can be described

Table 1.1 Household expenditures in Japan (my tabulation)

Item	*Amount*	*In USD*
Food	64,000	640
Housing	14,000	140
Fuel, light, water	30,000	300
Clothing, footwear	10,000	100
Medical care	13,000	130
Transport, communication	33,800	338
Education	12,200	122
Culture, recreation	28,000	280
Miscellaneous expenditures	61,000	610

as tourism while others suggest that tourism should be reserved for leisure activities. The World Tourism Organization, a branch of the United Nations, offers the following definition of tourism:

> It comprises the activities of persons traveling to and staying in places outside their usual environment for not more than one consecutive year for leisure, business, or other purposes not related to the exercise of an activity remunerated from within the place visited.

The word tourism comes from the Greek word *tournos*, which was a tool used to make a circle. Thus, the word tourist suggests making a circle, of sorts, by travelling somewhere and returning to the place from where one started.

This definition is too general, I believe, to deal with tourism – especially international tourism; so let me suggest some characteristics of international tourism that will help us gain a better understanding of this phenomenon. We must realize that tourism (around a 3.5 trillion industry in USD) is the largest industry in the world, having supplanted oil a number of years ago. The following list, which focuses on international tourism, is based on one in my book *Deconstructing Travel: Cultural Perspectives on Tourism* (AltaMira Press, 2004: 9) and is particularly applicable to packaged tours:

- It is *temporary*, for a relatively short period of time.
- It is *voluntary*, done by choice.
- It is done in *foreign* lands.
- It is tied to *leisure, pleasure* and *consumer culture*.
- It is *not involved in business* and earning money while abroad.
- It is based on a *round trip*, tied to a return to one's point of origin.
- It is made possible by *technological developments* in travel.
- It is a *mass phenomenon*, done by huge numbers of people.

All of these characteristics are of a general nature. Some people spend a year travelling around the world, but that is relatively uncommon. I do not consider business travellers to be the same kind of tourists as leisure travel tourists, although many business travellers have time when they are in foreign lands to be tourists and visit important sites, attend native entertainments and so on. There is a debate among tourism scholars about whether people who travel to a foreign country on business can be classified as tourists. I suggest that irrespective of how you might wish to classify business travellers, they too generally spend some time involved in activities connected with tourism.

In my 1986 visit to Japan, long before I thought of writing about tourism and Japanese culture and society, I listed (in my journal) a number of characteristics of tourists, experiences tourists often have and artefacts associated with tourism. They are given below:

- Maps
- Menus
- Guidebooks
- Currency conversion charts
- Seeing sights
- Chance encounters with others who speak the same language
- Dislocation and a lack of the sense of things
- Getting lost
- Walking endlessly
- Encountering the strange and exotic
- Unexpected expenses (but 'what the hell'.)
- Swapping information about places to visit

As I think about my travels since then, my list of things that tourists do and are preoccupied with has grown larger, but the list is still relevant. This is because tourists, wherever they are, face the same problems such as finding their way around, finding something to eat, diligently reading guidebooks to obtain information about the places they are visiting and trying to figure out the cost of things.

My wife and I were staying at the Yashima Ryokan in Shinjuku in 1986, where a breakfast of coffee, toast and an egg cost 250 yen ($1.50). We arrived in Japan early in the morning but were not allowed to go into our room until the afternoon, so we left our bags at the Ryokan and wandered around Shinjuku. The Ryokan cost around $33 for the two of us, so it was relatively cheap. It is still possible to stay in 'simple' Ryokans in Tokyo for around that price, but the fancier Ryokans now cost anything from $100 to several hundred dollars or more.

Popular Kinds of Tourism in Japan

Tourists have many interests when they travel, and thus different kinds of tourism have to be considered. They are not mutually exclusive, by any means. Below, I list and briefly describe some of the more important kinds of tourism and suggest some of the things that tourists see and do when they visit Japan. There are many different kinds of tourism – it is a highly segmented industry – but I have listed some of the more common kinds of tourism applicable to Japan.

Cultural tourism

Cultural tourists are interested in Japanese culture and visit museums, forts, shrines, castles, gardens and temples, attend musical and theatrical presentations, shop in Japanese stores and sample Japanese food. Their focus, then, is on what is distinctive and unique about Japanese culture. Typically, cultural tourists visit cities such as Tokyo and, more importantly, Kyoto, which is considered the most important city, culturally speaking, in Japan.

Adventure tourism

The focus of adventure tourists is on activities such as trekking in wilderness areas, climbing Mount Fuji, river rafting, and going to places that are off the beaten track. A soft form of adventure tourism involves bird watching and short walks in parks and natural reserves.

Ecotourism

Ecotourists typically visit countries where great attention is paid to preserving rain forests and natural reserves and where the government is sensitive to the natural environment. There are many forest areas in Japan that are of interest to ecotourists.

Family tourism

This involves attending weddings of friends or members of an extended family living in Japan and other life cycle events of people in Japan. Many Japanese citizens living in America return to Japan annually to visit their parents, siblings and relatives.

Food tourism

Because Japanese food is so distinctive, there are tours devoted to dining in great restaurants and learning how to purchase Japanese food products and cook Japanese food. Tokyo is now considered to have a larger number of the best, and most expensive, restaurants than any other city in the world, but the food in other parts of Japan is also very good. An American friend of mine who lived in Japan for 12 years once told me that if there was one thing she misses from her years there, it is the delicious food she got used to eating when she lived there.

Sex tourism

This is, unfortunately, an important and large component of the tourism industry everywhere, although Japan is not in the same league as Thailand. In addition to Japanese prostitutes, there are also a large number of

Photograph of author, wife and Sachiko in restaurant

prostitutes from the Philippines, Thailand and other countries. There are 'love' hotels found in the cities, which facilitate sexual encounters. In some cases, married men and women in Japan use these hotels because they do not have any privacy in their small flats.

Sports tourism

Sports tourists often go abroad for sports activities and, in the case of Japan, to ski, kayak, play golf and attend sports events such as baseball games and sumo wrestling. Japan also has excellent skiing facilities in its northern areas, and hosted a winter Olympics a number of years ago. Therefore, Japan attracts a number of tourists interested in sports activities of one kind or another.

Disaster tourism

This is a voyeuristic kind of tourism for people who want to visit disaster areas to see things for themselves and, in some cases, to help in any way they can. Thus, when there are devastating earthquakes in Japan, such as the one that occurred in Kobe, many disaster tourists, who can be understood as a special kind of voyeurs, visited Japan to see for themselves how much destruction there was and, in a curious way, 'participate' in history.

Because of the high cost of living in Japan and other factors, certain kinds of tourism, such as medical tourism and drug tourism, are not really important components of the tourism industry in Japan. Japan is not currently one of the most important international tourist destinations, but it is working hard to develop the tourism industry and the JNTO has a campaign to convince 10 million foreign tourists to visit the country in 2010.

One of the most popular activities tourists engage in involves shopping and there are many opportunities for foreign tourists to shop in Japan, which is one of the most well-developed consumer cultures. Data that I obtained from the JNTO on what American tourists do in Japan suggest that shopping is about as important as sightseeing.

The Imagined Japan, the 'Real' Japan and the Remembered Japan

The Mura quotation that opens this chapter, written by a Japanese American who spent a year there, shows a decided ambivalence about the country. The topics that Mura deals with reflect the way that many tourists feel about Japan, with its split between its highly developed traditional arts and its increasingly dominant popular culture. It is images that foreign tourists see in films, television and other media that help create an imagined Japan, the one many tourists seek, but when they get there they also find themselves immersed in a different Japan, the everyday Japan, that they must negotiate in their quest for their imagined Japan. The Pico Iyer quotation reflects the confusion and puzzled feelings that many tourists feel when they visit Japan because it is, in so many ways, different from the societies in which they live. I suggest that these feelings contribute to the sense of adventure tourists seek when they travel and make Japan an exciting destination, especially since Japan represents a safe adventure.

I suggest that travel to Japan, and foreign travel in general, involves three stages:

(1) *Imaginary Japan*: The imagined or pre-visualized trip.
(2) *Real Japan*: The experienced trip, as a tourist.
(3) *Remembered Japan*: The recollected trip, via journals, postcards, photographs, videos and souvenirs.

Why people decide to visit Japan, or any other foreign country, is difficult to determine. There could be any number of reasons: tourists who visit

Japan may like Japanese food, they may have seen the country in a film and have become interested or even 'enchanted' by it, they may be going to a conference there, they may know someone who visited the country and raved about how wonderful it was or there may be special 'deals' to travel there that they feel are too good to pass up. I am excluding from this list business matters, which also require a person to visit a foreign country. Of course, as pointed out earlier, in many cases people who travel to a country on business also spend some time there as a tourist.

Before we actually go to a country, we have an idea of what it is like and what kind of experiences we will have. At this stage, and I will use Japan as the country we are visiting, we have an imaginary or pre-visualized Japan. Many tourists purchase guidebooks to find out more about the country – to learn something about the hotels, the food, the customs and the 'hot' restaurants, and to see photographs of important sites and things to do, among other things. I believe the images we see of Japan enable us to visualize ourselves doing various things there and play an important role in our decision to go there and help determine many of the things we do.

In his book *The Art of Travel*, Alain de Botton's first chapter is titled 'On Anticipation', and recounts how the nasty weather in London made him (2002: 8) 'intensely susceptible to the unsolicited arrival of a large, brightly illustrated brochure entitled "Winter Sun"', which had a row of palm trees on a sandy beach. He adds:

> The longing provoked by the brochure was an example, at once touching and bathetic, of how projects (and even whole lives) might be influenced by the simplest and most unexamined images of happiness; of how a lengthy and ridiculously expensive journey might be set in motion by nothing more than the sight of a photograph of a palm tree gently inclining in a tropical breeze.
>
> I resolved to travel to the island of Barbados. (Botton, 2002: 8, 9)

When he gets there, he speculates about the fact that he had not thought very much about having to get to his destination and that sometimes what we find when we get to a destination is not what we anticipated. It is our anticipation of the pleasures we will experience in Japan or any other country, reinforced by the picture-filled brochures and the fact-filled guidebooks we obtain about the country, that leads us to travel there.

The second stage involves actually going to Japan and travelling around in the country, seeing the important temples, gardens, forts, museums and other sites of touristic interest. As a tourist, you may sample the different Japanese foods, look around for things to purchase, attend a sumo wrestling match or go to a theatrical presentation. If you are on a packaged tour, the company selects an itinerary that covers some of the more important sites to visit. If you are a lone traveller, you will probably have compiled a list of places to go to and things to do. Most tourists take numerous photographs and may also make videos of the places they go to, the things they do and the people they meet. The digital camera (and increasingly the video camera) is now almost ubiquitous among tourists, who seek to document their experiences and capture images that will help them recall the trip.

The third stage involves the recollected trip and may involve notes in journals, in some cases travel videos. This stage generally involves many digitally photographed images that are printed by a variety of means, such as home printers, internet photo services or local drugstores (where you can take your digital card and have photos made). Tourists often put these photos in large books that help them recall the trip. In addition, many people load these images into their computers and have them flash on the screen as screen savers or purchase video frames that use digital cards to offer slide-show images from their trip.

Not only do people usually spend a good deal of time before taking a trip investigating the country, so that they do not miss anything important, they also devote a considerable amount of time after a trip looking at the videos and photographs they have taken and remembering the high points of their trip. Photography plays a major role in the tourist experience, and some social scientists have suggested that many tourists are so preoccupied with taking photos that they do not enjoy or really see the places they go to. It has also been suggested that the choice of sites that tourists visit is affected, to a considerable extent, by the photo opportunities the sites provide.

Social-psychologist Stanley Milgram argues, in an article titled 'The Image Freezing Machine' (*Society*, November/December 1976) suggests that tourists must always make a trade-off between enjoying a place and photographing it and that tourism has been transformed, thanks to the digital camera and video camera, because of the way people in foreign lands seek out photo opportunities. Arriving at a desired place, such as the Golden Pavilion in Kyoto, photographing it becomes more important for some tourists than actually looking at and experiencing the temple.

Many tourists evaluate their vacations on the basis of the great photographs that they were able to take of important iconic tourist destinations. They often put themselves or their wives and family in these photographs to document the fact that they actually were at a temple in Kyoto or in Asakusa for the Sanja Matsuri festival.

The development of digital cameras and digital video cameras now makes taking photos and making videos easier; hence, tourists can now

Photograph of Golden Pavilion

take photographs of sites they visit without having to do more than point and shoot. It is so easy for tourists to take digital photographs and dispose of images that they do not like that sometimes they take 10 or 20 shots of the sites they visit so that they get at least one or two 'great' photographs.

Guidebook Perspectives on Japan

It is useful to see how guidebooks portray Japan. To do this, I have selected the first paragraph (or the first few hundred words when the first paragraph is short or requires more text for amplification) from a number of guidebooks to Japan. These first paragraphs have the function of selling the country, and the guidebook, to readers. But they also have to give readers some sense of what the country is like. Therefore, it is instructive to examine these passages in the guidebooks to see whether they have anything in common. I will start with *The National Geographic Traveler Japan*. The first paragraph in this guidebook reads as follows:

FIRST THERE IS JAPAN THE ARCHIPELAGO. IT'S A NARROW CHAIN ALONG THE Asian mainland stretching some 1,860 miles (2994 km) from eastern Siberia down almost to Taiwan. North to south, Hokkaido, Honshu, Shikoku, and Kyushu are the four largest islands; the whole is administratively divided into 47 prefectures. Then there is Japan the concept. Chances are you're already familiar with the traditional icons – Buddhist temples, flower arrangements and gardens, the kimono, and martial arts. You've probably eaten sushi, played computer games, and either used or endured karaoke; you know that many of the products and components involved in your daily communication, entertainment, and transport are made in Japan. So most visitors pose themselves the question long before they get there: Which is the real Japan?

Everyone knows the hackneyed calendar image of snowcapped Fuji-san at cherry blossom time with the sleep bullet train streaking past – perhaps with a kimono girl in the foreground. A Japanese invention, the image symbolizes how the Japanese see themselves. As they never tire of pointing out (along with the fact that they have four seasons), ancient arts, crafts and traditions coexist in harmony with the cutting edge of modern technological civilization. As different as the component parts may seem, they're *all* the real Japan. (Bornoff, 2000: 10)

This guide, published by the National Geographic, starts with a geographic description of Japan. Although we tend to think of Japan as a small country, it is actually larger than Great Britain. Bornoff poses a question that travellers in all countries ask themselves – am I seeing 'authentic' Japan, that is, 'the real thing?' His answer is that there are two Japans: the ancient Japan of forts, kimonos and sumo wrestlers and the modern Japan of new technology gizmos, gleaming skyscrapers and neon-lit downtown areas in cities such as Tokyo.

This 'schizoid' aspect of Japan is featured in our second guidebook, Simon Richmond and Jan Dodd's *The Rough Guide to Japan*:

For a country that lived in self-imposed isolation until 150 years ago, Japan has not hesitated in making up for lost time since the world came calling. Anyone who's eaten sushi or used a Sony Walkman feels they know something about this slinky archipelago of some 6800 volcanic islands and yet, from the moment of arrival in this oddly familiar, quintessentially oriental land it's almost as if you've touched down on another planet.

Japan is a place of ancient gods and customs, but it is also the cutting edge of cool modernity. High-speed trains whisk you from one end of the country to another with frightening punctuality. You can catch sight of a farmer tending his paddy field, then turn the corner and find yourself next to a neon-festooned electronic games parlour in the suburb of a sprawling metropolis. One day you could be picking through the fashions in the biggest department store on earth, the next relaxing in an outdoor hot-spring pool, watching cherry blossoms or snowflakes fall, depending on the season. (Richmond & Dodd, 2005: iii)

The authors of this guide also focus on the two different Japans – the Japan of the ancients and the modern and postmodern Japan of the present day. They also point out something that has been very important in the development of Japanese culture and national character, namely that Japan was isolated from the world for a number of centuries and has only been involved with the outside world for the past 150 years.

The next guide is the *DK Eyewitness Travel Guide: Japan*, published in 2000, Japan. In the section titled 'A Portrait of Japan', we read:

Few people in the modern world are not affected in some way by the ideas, culture, and economy of Japan, yet this country remains for many an enigma, an unsolved riddle. Westernized, but different from any Western country, part of Asia, but clearly unlike any other Asian country, Japan is a uniquely adaptable place where tradition and modernity are part of one continuum.

With over 3,000 islands lying along the Pacific Ring of Fire, the Japanese archipelago is prone to frequent earthquakes and has 60 active volcanoes. Much of the country is mountainous, while cities consume large areas of the flat land and coastal plain. The Tokyo-Yokahama area is the largest urban concentration in the world, and 70 percent of Japan's 125 million people live along the Pacific coast stretch between Tokyo and Kyushu. (Thiro, 2000)

What this introduction adds to the discussion involves several things. First, it focuses on Japan's uniqueness, its exceptionalism and its enigmatic nature, on the fact that it is Western in its own distinctive manner and that, while it is Asian, it is not like any other Asian country. In addition, we learn that the Tokyo–Yokahama conurbation is the largest one in the world, which explains why the places that most tourists visit in Japan are so crowded with people.

Our final guide is a Japanese one (in the English language) published by Kodansha International, Ian L. McQueen's *Japan: A Budget Travel Guide*:

Japan is one of the most interesting of all countries to visit. It has a long history, with many remains from past periods, like magnificent temples and castles, yet it is possibly the most dynamically modern country on earth, with an incredible amount of industrialization (very much a mixed blessing). Its historic culture and society were completely different from anything known in the west, and many attitudes formed in the far past affect life today. Festivals from centuries ago are still held, linking present with past. Despite the 'exotic' element of the country, however, it is one of the most accessible in terms of good transportation, plentiful accommodation, and friendly people, with no risk of eating bad food nor of personal danger.

Thousands of western travellers go to Japan every year (along with several times as many Asians from nearby countries), but only a relative few venture outside Tokyo, Kyoto, and a couple of other well-trod tourist destinations. There is nothing wrong with spending time in these places, of course, for they do house many of the country's chief attractions, but those who venture a little off the beaten path will find that they are in a country where foreigners are still quite a rare sight outside the major population centers, and the people are friendly. It is not like the outer reaches of a Himalayan kingdom, for example, scarcely known to the outside world, yet an element of discovery is still possible. (McQueen, 1997)

This passage is the one with the most direct appeal to tourists, suggesting reasons as to why they should consider travelling in Japan. It is similar to the other passages quoted in pointing out the link between Japan's feudal past and its modern present. The author mentions the so-called 'exotic' quality of Japan, which he sees as very positive, and argues that 'exotic' Japan is easily available to tourists since Japan's tourism infrastructure is so well-developed. He also suggests that there are many parts of Japan worth visiting where tourists do not conventionally go – places where tourists can escape from the traditional places they tend to visit and where discovery is still possible.

All of these guidebooks present their readers with a fairly similar picture of Japan, as a place where ancient traditions and modernity are all mixed together and the result is something enticing, enigmatic and 'exotic', a term usually applied to countries such as India or Thailand. Tourists who visit countries such as Japan generally only see certain things of interest to tourists, yet, if they spend any time in Tokyo and Kyoto, they cannot help but be exposed to various aspects of Japanese everyday life. They will see children in their school uniforms, eat Japanese food of all kinds, notice *Pachinko* parlours (and maybe even try their hand at it) and see salarymen. They will see the Japanese flag, notice all the manga bookstores, attend sumo wrestling matches and baseball games, and participate in other aspects of Japanese popular and high culture. They may, if they listen to Ian McQueen, venture into areas not generally considered to be tourist spaces and have 'real' adventures.

Japanese National Character

The Japanese, as the Pico Iyer quotation at the beginning of this chapter suggests, are 'different'. As a result of historical experiences, including Japan's isolation from the rest of the world for a number of centuries, and as a consequence of Japan's geography, an island with a large population and relatively little land for the size of its population, the Japanese have developed a distinctive culture. This culture is a reflection of, and perhaps also affected by, what we can describe as the Japanese national character. Although there are regional differences in Japan, it is reasonable to argue that there is such a thing as 'Japanese national character', which refers to the values, beliefs, codes of conduct and practices that are commonly accepted there.

A British scholar, Geoffrey Gorer (1943), speculated in an article 'Themes in Japanese Culture' that the Japanese are preoccupied with tidiness, with ritual and with orderliness. This, he suggested, was similar to the behaviour of obsessive compulsive people and was caused by the severity of toilet training of Japanese children, which led to unconscious and repressed aggressive feelings. Another scholar, Weston La Barre, in a paper 'Some Observations on Character Structure in the Orient: The Japanese', listed the various compulsive traits he found in Japanese people:

> ... secretiveness, hiding of emotions and attitudes; perseveration and persistency; conscientiousness; self-righteousness; a tendency to project attitudes; fanaticism; arrogance; 'touchiness'; precision and perfectionism; neatness and ritualistic cleanliness; ceremoniousness; conformity to rule; sadomasochistic behavior; hypochondriasis; suspiciousness; jealousy and enviousness; pedantry; sentimentality; love of scatological obscenity and anal sexuality. (La Barre, 1945: 326)

La Barre also attributed these characteristics to early toilet training, although neither he nor Gorer had any evidence that Japanese children experience 'severe' toilet training and other studies suggest that toilet training in Japan is not that different, generally speaking, from toilet training in the United States.

Richard K. Beardsley argued in his book *Twelve Doors to Japan* that:

> Few areas of comparable population anywhere in the world have such culturally homogenous people who were so long isolated from other peoples.... In isolation the Japanese missed what most people have

experienced, a constant rubbing of elbows with outsiders. (Beardsley, 1965: 360)

It is their isolation that makes it easy to understand why the Japanese were able to develop such a distinctive way of life. One of the most significant aspects of Japanese life involves sleeping arrangements. It is not unusual for children in Japan to sleep with their parents until they are 10 years old, and in many cases even older, although older sons tend to sleep alone.

In their article 'Who Sleeps by Whom? Parent–Child Involvement in Urban Japanese Families', William Caudill and David W. Plath write:

> ... Sleeping arrangements in Japanese families tend to blur the distinction between generations and between the sexes, to emphasize the interdependence more than the separateness of individuals, and to underplay (or largely ignore) the potentiality for conjugal intimacy between husband and wife in sexual and other matters in favor of a more general familial cohesion. (Caudill & Plath, 1966: 344–366)

This kind of sleeping arrangement inhibits sexual activity and intimacy between husbands and wives. Recent studies have shown that relatively large numbers of married men and women in Japan have little or no sexual intercourse nowadays. The design of Japanese houses and the lack of room in many of them may play an important role in sleeping arrangements and sexual behaviour.

Japanese parents are said to be incredibly indulgent towards their children. There are conflicting opinions about whether Japanese children are 'spoiled' and whether Japanese boys are often aggressive and rude in the way they treat their mothers. It is not unusual for mothers in such situations to slap their children. Children are under a great deal of pressure to do well in school (I will deal with school children and their problems later in the book) and according to Geoffrey Gorer and Ruth Benedict, 'when a teacher sends a bad report about the child, the family turns against the child' (Barnouw, 1973: 231). A number of scholars in the 1970s argued that Japanese children bore the burden of a powerful sense of responsibility, obligation and a need for achievement that led to incredible tension – an underlying excitability that the Japanese hold in check by their orderliness.

Doctrinaire Freudians might describe the basic Japanese character as having 'anal erotic' tendencies. As Freud (1963) wrote in his 1908 essay 'Character and Anal Eroticism', anal erotics are exceptionally *'orderly, parsimonious,* and *obstinate'* (quoted in Philip Rieff, ed., *Freud: Character and Culture*).

Freud's ideas about anal eroticism and toilet training may have influenced the writings by Geoffrey Gorer and Weston La Barre quoted earlier.

Much of this discussion of national character is based on works described by Victor Barnouw in his book *Culture and Personality*, published in 1973. Although the research described in this book is mostly from the 1940s and 1950s, there is reason to suggest that national character does not change that much over the years and decades even though a society may experience considerable social change. It is useful to keep these theories about Japanese national character in mind when one travels in Japan and observes what is going on there.

In 'Japan and China: National Character Writ Large', Norimitsu Onishi explains that Japan is unique in the world in having a language, katakana, to depict foreign words and names, thus indicating the non-Japanese nature of people and things. We read:

> Of all languages in the world, Japanese is the only one that has an entirely different set of written characters to express foreign words and names. Just seeing these characters automatically tells the Japanese that they are dealing with something or someone non-Japanese. (Onishi, 2004)

The Japanese, Onishi writes, have four different sets of characters they use in their writing:

Kanji	Chinese characters
Hirigana	Phonetic characters for Japanese words
Katatana	Phonetic characters for foreign words
English	Romanji

Japan, Onishi suggests, is inner-looking and exclusionary and uneasy about foreigners and foreign influences, although as the Japanese travel more and are exposed to other cultures, their attitudes are slowly changing. The Japanese language, with its different alphabets, reinforces the tendency the Japanese have to divide the world into people and things that are Japanese and everything and everyone else.

This may be connected, I believe, to their attitudes about purity and their desire to maintain a distinctive Japanese culture. I should add that some letters to the *New York Times* disputed some of Onishi's contentions. The attitudes that the Japanese have about racial purity and their reluctance to import workers from foreign countries are posing a serious problem for Japan. The Japanese birth rate is very low and the Japanese population is aging, so the country is running out of workers.

〈参観許可書をお持ちでない方〉
参観には許可書が必要です。
参観を希望される方は、宮内庁京都事務所へお申し込みください。
当日の参観はできません。

A permit for visit is required.
Please apply to Imperial Household Agency Kyoto Office.
Walk—in visitors are not accepted.

【電話／Telephone】 ０７５－２１１－１２１５

Different kinds of Japanese writing

As Masaru Tamamoto, a Senior Fellow at the World Policy Institute, writes in his article 'Japan's Crisis of the Mind':

> If we want to survive as a nation, we must shed our deeply rooted resistance to immigration. Contrary to widespread prejudices in favor of keeping Japan 'pure', we desperately need to dilute our blood. Our aging nation will need millions of university-educated middle-class immigrants with high productivity, people who will put down roots and raise families, whose pride and success will be the affirmation of new Japanese values. (Masaru Tamamoto, 2009: A21)

If Japan does not change its policies towards immigration and find new leadership, he adds, its economy will continue to decline and the quality of life of the Japanese people will deteriorate even more.

In my first journal about Japan, written during our visit there in 1986, I listed some aspects of Japanese culture and society that interested me and attracted my attention. This list is reproduced below.

Miniaturization	Sumo wrestlers
Hyper-modernism	The Japanese aesthetic
Lingering medievalism	Alcoholism
Expensive	Stress and pressure
Uniformity	Pagan, non-Puritanical
Squat toilets	Shame culture?
Sense of place	Organization
Work ethic	Conscientiousness

I had written a portion of this book when I found my journal covering our trip to Japan, and what strikes me, as I think about this list, is how many of the topics I listed in 1986 are the ones that I wrote about in this book, more than 20 years later.

John Gunther and Stereotypes of the Japanese

Stereotypes are group-shared and over-simplified images people have about what individuals who are members of other races, religions, and ethnic and other kinds of groups and nationalities are like. The stereotypes can be positive, negative or neutral, but in all cases they represent gross simplifications and do not take into account differences in individuals who are members of the groups that are stereotyped. In the case of the Japanese, we can find both positive and negative stereotypes that are quite common.

What often happens is that people generalize from their experiences with one member of some group to all the members of that group. In addition, stereotypes pervade the mass media because they provide those who make films, television commercials and other mass-mediated texts, shortcuts to motivation in characters. Many stereotypes involve visual phenomena, such as skin colour, hair colour and nose shape. Another important thing to recognize about stereotypes is that often they contain a grain of truth to them, even if they are overgeneralizations. I can think of no better source of stereotypes about the Japanese people than those found in John Gunther's (1938) *Inside Asia* and in a companion volume to his earlier book, *Inside Europe*. Gunther devotes the first eight chapters of *Inside Asia* to Japan. In his second chapter, 'First Course in Japanese', he contrasts Japanese and Chinese culture and offers a number of descriptions of Chinese and Japanese character and culture.

Generally speaking, Gunther is positive about the Chinese and rather negative about the Japanese, but not always. We must keep in mind that this book was published in 1939 and thus reflects stereotypes that were common at that time. What is interesting about these stereotypes is that many of them are still current, in part, because of the way Japanese people are portrayed in the mass media. In recent years, as Japanese culture and society have changed, many of Gunther's observations are no longer valid – that is, if they ever were valid.

I will offer a selection of short quotations from his chapter that deals with the Japanese culture and personality and the Japanese national character and indicate the page numbers where I found the material I am quoting.

Page 28:

Most Japanese are short and squat … Many Japanese have thick, pouting lips … Japanese suck in breath sharply when they talk to superiors and foreigners, a kind of hiss, which is intended to demonstrate respect … The Japanese love to drink and get drunk easily, especially on beer. The Japanese love color in clothes … The Japanese are very good at sports, like baseball and tennis. The Japanese buy goods 90% made in Japan.

Page 29:

The Japanese love Chinese food … The Japanese do not mean much when they smile … The Japanese possess those virtues which a cynic might consider rather dull: industriousness and an exaggerated tendency to hygiene … The Japanese never smoke opium. But they make money selling it to the Chinese … The Japanese are fanatics … It would be hard to tell whether the Japanese despise the Chinese more than the Chinese despise the Japanese.

In this chapter, Gunther compares the Japanese with the Chinese and is much more positive about the Chinese people than about the Japanese people.

He admits that it is 'risky' to deal with national character, but decides to write about it anyway, discussing what he sees as distinctive Japanese traits.

Page 30:

The Japanese are a prickly and difficult people. Japanese character is full of paradox.

Page 31:

Japanese patriotism is to a certain extent a function of Shinto, which teaches that the country is a single family, a unit … Japanese sense of detail includes the smallest items … The Japanese have an almost unique sense of national discipline, an inheritance of the Samurai tradition, which emphasizes conformity and solidarity; to a great extent they are creatures of convention … The Japanese cannot endure demonstration of lack of discipline … Another essay might be written on Japanese inventiveness and ingeniousness, which are considerable. The Japanese are not only good mimics, as is notorious; they have a very direct and original practicality … Many Japanese lack grace; many seem to lack poise, charm, tolerance, and a sense of humor … It is impossible to deny Japanese stoicism and courage.

Page 32:

Japanese brothels are the most extensive in the world; thousands upon thousands of young girls – even children – are sold into prostitution by their parents every year; and the kind of professional hostess known as the Geisha is a distinctive feature of Japanese life. There is little odium attached to prostitution in Japan.

Page 33:

The Japanese are incredibly touchy, which may be partly a result of diet. They eat too much iodine in the shape of raw fish, and their thyroids are overdeveloped.

It took Gunther two years to write his book and he informs us, in a note at the beginning of the book, that he had been to the Near East, as it was called then, four times as a war correspondent for the *Chicago Daily News* and visited every country he discusses in his book. In this note, he ends by calling Japan 'a powerful and dangerous nation' and mentioning that the war that Japan was waging in China was connected to the war being waged by Germany and Italy in Europe. He added that Japan was an ally of Germany and Italy and suggested that a 'general conflagration' was coming, in which Japan, the subject of around half the chapters in *Inside Asia*, would play a major role.

A book edited by Takie Sugiyama Lebra and William P. Libra, *Japanese Culture and Behavior: Selected Readings,* offers articles that counter the simplistic characterizations of Japanese people and Japanese national character made by Gunther and other writers. A number of articles in the book argue that the picture of the Japanese as dominated by groups and seeking harmony and trying to avoid conflict is not correct, although this matter is the subject of considerable debate among those who study Japanese culture.

Sociologists of modern Japan are, of course, dealing with a different society from the one that Gunther wrote about in 1939. There are now serious problems with the Hikikomori (young recluses) in Japan; there are the Shinjinrui – gangs of youth that are alienated and anomic, and the iconic Salaryman is fading away as a cultural archetype, just like the Geisha, who is in many respects his opposite. These topics will be discussed in the second part of this book.

It is reasonable to assume that when tourists decide upon Japan as a destination, they have certain notions about what they will find in Japan and what spending time among the Japanese will be like. Many of these notions are fuelled by images of Japan that people might see in travel literature, in films or read about in books that deal with Japan – fiction and non-fiction. Certain aspects of life in Japan are very positive for tourists. For instance, Japan is an extremely safe country to visit. Another factor is the legendary – should we add stereotyped notion – about the Japanese being, as a rule, very courteous and helpful to tourists. This means that tourists in Japan will not have the same kind of experiences that they would have in some highly touristed countries such as France and Spain, where many of the inhabitants have become upset regarding the number of tourists in their country – both foreign and domestic – and are often hostile to them.

Some Tours of Japan

At this point, it is useful to examine where American tourists generally go and what do they do when they take package tours of Japan. Many tourists, not on package tours, probably approximate the tours that are described below. Tours of Japan are considerably more expensive than tours of other 'exotic' countries, such as Thailand, India or Vietnam. Below I offer some examples of standard group tours of Japan from companies at different price levels.

Luxury tour of Japan	*Budget tour of Japan*
Tauck tours	Intrepid tours
12 days from $5,790	14 Days $1895 (+$600)
Airfare not included (add around $950)	Airfare not included (add around $950)

Itinerary	*Itinerary*
1. Arrive in Tokyo	1. Tokyo
2. Discover Tokyo	2. Tokyo
3. Ginza/Senso-Ji Temple	3. Tokyo
4. Fuji-Hakone National Park	4. Hakone
5. Hakone/Japanese Alps	5. Hakone
6. Historic Takayama	6. Takayama
7. Shirakawa-Go/Ryokan	7. Takayama
8. Kanazawa/Kyoto	8. Hiroshima

Itinerary	*Itinerary*
9. Enchanting Kyoto	9. Hiroshima
10. Tranquil Nara	10. Hiroshima
11. A day at leisure in Kyoto	11. Kyoto
12. Journey home	12. Kyoto
	13. Kyoto
	14. Return from Kyoto

The Intrepid tour requires everyone to purchase, on their own, a 14-day Japan Rail Pass, which adds $414 to the price of the tour and those taking the tour must also pay a $200 local payment and spend around $200 for meals not included in the tour, which means the Intrepid tour ends up costing around $2500. It is less than half as much as the Tauck tour, which is a luxury tour. The Tauck tour includes 11 breakfasts, seven lunches and seven dinners, and the people on the tour stay at fancy hotels. On the other hand, some times the Tauck tour has as many as 26 people while the Intrepid tours have a maximum group size of 12 people. Most of the tours of Japan provided by travel agencies fall within the range of Tauck and Intrepid tours.

Smartours has a 12-day 'Discover Japan' tour for $2699, which is similar to many of the other tours in that it visits Tokyo, Mt. Fuji, Hakone, Takayama, Kanazawa and Kyoto. The Tokyo (and environs), Takayama, Kanazawa and Kyoto itinerary is one of the most common ones used in group tours of Japan. The price does not include extra fees charged by airline companies.

To see how expensive tours of Japan are, you can compare both the Tauck and the Intrepid tours of Japan with a Gate 1 tour of Thailand, which includes round trips from Los Angeles and costs from $1199 per person (and up to $1499, depending on the time the tour is taken and when travellers book their tours) for 12 days. The airfare from the United States to Japan is not expensive but hotels, restaurants and transportation are relatively expensive, especially when compared with other 'exotic' countries such as Thailand and Vietnam.

On the other hand, there are many budget hotels in Japan, such as Toyoko Inns, that are simple but reasonable and Japanese restaurants often have moderately priced set meals; so it is possible to travel in Japan, if one is careful, and not spend a fortune. One way of doing this is to check out comments on Japan at websites such as Virtual Tourist, Frommer's 'Travel Talk', the Lonely Planet's 'Thorn Tree' and at the websites of the Japan National Tourist Organization and various Japanese websites for hotels, ryokans and minshukus.

A Suggested Itinerary of Japan

A young Japanese sociologist, Naomi Chiba, with whom I have corresponded over the years, provided her suggestions for a tour of Japan for those who wish to tour Japan on their own or who wish to check this suggested itinerary with those offered by tour companies in which they are interested:

Tokyo (Tokyo to)

- General Tokyo Tourist Information (updated 1 April 2008): http://www.tourism.metro.tokyo.jp/english/
- Imperial Palace
- Ginza–Kabukiza–Tsukiji–Odaiba
- Yasukuni Shrine (The shrine enshrines war dead and class A war criminals)
- Asakusa: http://www.japan-guide.com/e/e3001.html
- Tokyo Tower: http://www.tokyotower.co.jp/333/foreign/eng/index.html
- Roppongi: http://www.roppongihills.com/en/
- Meiji Jingu (The shrine enshrines the Meiji emperor)
- Harajuku Area
- Shibuya Area
- Shinjuku Area

Kamakura (Kanagawa prefecture)

- The Giant Buddha of Kamakura (Kamakura Daibutsu)
- Tsurugaoka Hachimangu Shrine
- Engakuji Temple
- Kamakura beach

Hakone (Kanagawa prefecture)

- Mt. Fuji (Fuji-san)
- Owakudani Hot Springs: http://www.owakudani.com/modules/mw_top/index.php?ml_lang=en
- Lake Ashi (Ashi no ko)
- Hakone Open Air Museum

Nikko (Tochigi prefecture)

- Shrines and temples in Nikko have been inscribed on the World Heritage List: http://whc.unesco.org/en/list/913
- Toshogu Shrine
- Rinnoji Temple

- Edo Wonderland (An amusement part, Nikko Edo Mura in Japanese): http://www.edowonderland.net/home.html

Takayama (Gifu prefecture)

- Historic Villages of Shirakawa-go and Gokayama. (Properties have been inscribed on the World Heritage List: http://whc.unesco.org/en/list/734)
- Detail maps and event information around this area from Japan National Tourist Organization: http://www.jnto.go.jp/eng/location/rtg/pdf/pg-409.pdf#search='takayama'

Kyoto (Kyoto fu)

- There are many historical and beautiful places in Kyoto. There are many seasonal festivals, especially Aoi matsuri in spring. Properties of historic monuments of ancient Kyoto (Kyoto, Uji and Otsu Cities) have been inscribed on the World Heritage List: http://whc.unesco.org/en/list/688
- Kiyomizu Temple
- Heian Shrine (It enshrines the Koumei emperor)
- The Golden Pavilion (Kinkakuji)
- Byodo-in (The temple is inscribed on a 10-yen Japanese coin)
- Daikakuji (Temple in Saga area): http://www.daikakuji.or.jp/
- Daikakuji English: http://www.daikakuji.or.jp/english/index.html
- Ginkakuji (Temple)
- Nanzenji (Temple)

Nara (Nara prefecture)

- Properties of Buddhist monuments in the Horyu-ji area have been inscribed on the World Heritage List: http://whc.unesco.org/en/list/660

Himeji (Hyogo prefecture)

- Himeji Castle (The property has been inscribed on the World Heritage List)

Hiroshima

- Aki-no-Miyajima Area (It has been inscribed on the World Heritage List)
- Itsukushima jinja (The Shinto shrine has been inscribed on the World Heritage List: http://whc.unesco.org/en/list/776): http://www.iwaso.com/e_introduction.html

- Hiroshima Peace Memorial Park (Genbaku Dome in Japanese. The property has been inscribed on the World Heritage List)
- Peace Memorial Park Museum (Heiwa Kinen Koen Shiryo-kan)
- Hiroshima Castle
- Shukkeien (a Japanese garden)

The Japan National Tourist Organization's Japan

The website of the JNTO is full of wonderful information. You can spend hours looking at different things it has to offer. One topic it deals with is the Japanese culture and it lists a number of important things to see and do to experience what is distinctive about this culture:

Japanese architecture	Ryokans
Shinto shrines	En-nichi (street fairs)
Calligraphy	Lacquer ware
Pottery	Communal baths
Gardens	Castles
Buddhist temples	Tea ceremony
Floral art	Bonsai
Sumo wrestling	Geishas
Typical foods	Ginza and other districts

In this book, I will deal with some of these topics and others that I think are of importance for tourists. When we travel to a foreign country, we look for experiences that are different from the ones we have in our native country.

One reason we travel is to get away from our everyday routines and recharge our batteries, so to speak. We want to see different architecture, buy souvenirs, sample different foods, and although we have probably eaten in many Japanese restaurants, we want to see whether they are different in Japan. Whatever one might want to say about Japan, one thing is certain – it has a distinctive culture and is different from other countries. It provides certain gratifications for tourists that they are looking for, which explains why so many tourists who visit Japan find it so 'enchanting' and delightful a country.

Uses and Gratifications of Tourism in Japan

In this discussion, I will employ a methodology that many media researchers developed to help understand why people watch certain television programmes, listen to certain radio programmes, read certain kinds of books (such as romance novels) and purchase various kinds of entertainments. Instead of focusing on the effects of media on audiences, the uses and gratifications methodology deals with the uses people make of media and the gratifications that the media provide them. Much of this research has been done by asking people about their media preferences and trying to determine what gratifications these preferences provide them. I will use the 'uses and gratifications' methodology to discuss Japan as a tourism destination and list some of the more important uses and gratifications of travel in Japan.

To be amused and entertained

Many tourists visit Japan because they believe that being in such a distinctive and unique culture will provide them with various kinds of pleasure and that they will find their trip entertaining and enriching. They will dine in Japanese restaurants and may also attend Japanese cultural events such as sumo wrestling matches and Noh dramas and find the nightlife in Tokyo and other cities exciting. There are also beautiful gardens and remarkable forts to visit, along with museums and other sites of interest.

To experience the beautiful

Japan has many beautiful parks and other natural areas that delight tourists. They may travel to Mount Fuji (and even climb it) or they may visit the inland sea. There is also a very distinctive Japanese aesthetic, as found in its food, dress, architecture, gardens, means of flower arranging, many of its products and various other aspects of Japanese life and culture.

To satisfy our curiosity

One reason why people visit a country is because they are curious about it and want to explore it and come to their own conclusions about it. Because Japan has such a distinctive culture, it generates curiosity in people who are thinking of visiting it and want to see things for themselves and try to figure out what makes Japanese culture 'tick'.

Photograph of Japanese garden

To participate in history

Tourism is a form of time travel. When tourists visit ancient forts, shrines and temples in Japan, they travel back in time to when they were built. In a sense, they are participating in history. There are also many monuments of contemporary significance, such as those found in Hiroshima commemorating the day when the United States dropped an atomic bomb on the city. Japan was an enemy of the United States in the Second World War, so it has a historic importance to Americans and plays a role in our historic imagination that many other countries do not have.

To help reinforce national identity

The Swiss linguist Ferdinand de Saussure, one of the founders of semiotics, said that concepts do not have any meaning in themselves. Their meaning comes from their relations with other concepts – the most important of those being opposition. As he explained, 'concepts are purely differential and defined not by their positive content but negatively by their relations with the other terms of the system. Their most precise characteristic is in being what the others are not ...' (Saussure, 1966: 117). What this means, as far as tourism is concerned, is that we find out who we are by seeing how we are different from others. Thus, one of the reasons we travel is to find out more about ourselves by comparing ourselves with others, and Japan is much more different from American culture than are England and other European countries, although each country is distinctive and helps tourists in foreign lands consolidate their identities.

To obtain a sense of community with others

Wherever you travel, you find that there are many kind people and that people, in every country, are often friendly and go out of their way to be helpful. Thus, travel helps people gain a sense of fellowship with others, wherever they travel. When people from other countries visit a country with as distinctive a culture as Japan, they still find that despite the differences in the way Japanese live and do things, tourists discover that they have many things in common with the Japanese people.

In an article in the Sunday *San Francisco Chronicle* (10 February 2008: D3) that dealt with a trip he made to Japan, John Flinn, discusses the help that various Japanese people gave him when an express train from Kyoto to the Kansai International Airport near Osaka was cancelled. A railway worker saw he was standing on the train platform and had a duffel bag, so the railway worker asked 'Kansai'? Flinn nodded. Then the worker ran to his office and came back a few minutes later holding a cell phone connected to one of the few English-speaking workers on duty that day. She explained that there had been an accident and the train had been cancelled, but she told him that he could still make it to the airport on time by taking a number of local trains.

The railway worker escorted Flinn to the platform for the local train and explained the situation to a businessman on the local train. He, in turn, discussed Flinn's predicament with other passengers. One person after another looked after Flinn. 'For the next hour', he writes, 'I was handed off like a relay baton from helper to helper until I arrived at Kansai airport, where I made my flight with seconds to spare. Not a word of English was exchanged, just many bows, smiles and *arigatos* (thank-yous) on my part'. Flinn concludes that this experience was one of his 'fondest and most vivid' memories of Japan. He adds that all independent travellers have experiences like this.

To renew oneself (recharge one's batteries)

Everyday life is based on routines and habits and continues on, with minor changes, endlessly. Psychologists have found that it is important for people to get away from their work and everyday routines and to 'recharge' their batteries, so to speak. One thing about vacations is that they are time-bound and an interruption into our everyday routines. When we travel abroad, we have adventures, we see how other people live, we try different foods and we focus on pleasure and enjoyment.

The German sociologist Georg Simmel wrote an essay, 'The Adventure', which offers us some insights into the value of travel. He wrote:

> The most general form of adventure is its dropping out of the continuity of life. 'Wholeness of Life', after all, refers to the fact that a consistent process runs through the individual components of life, however crassly and irreconcilably distinct they may be. What we call an adventure stands in contrast to that interlocking of life-links, to that feeling that those counter-currents, turnings, and knots still, after all, spin forth a continuous thread ... We ascribe to an adventure a beginning and an end much sharper that those to be discovered in other forms of our experiences. (quoted in David Frisby and Mike Featherstone, eds, *Simmel on Culture*, 1997: 222)

Simmel's ideas about adventures explain why travel is so life-enhancing and pleasurable, for when we are tourists we become adventurers (even if our adventures are 'soft' and generally not terribly challenging) and we escape from the mundane routines of everyday life, if only for a short while. Adventures, Simmel adds, take on the quality of dreams, which may explain to the pleasant memories we have of our travels.

Conclusions

Tourism is more than an 'escape' attempt from our everyday lives; it is really one of the last opportunities for people to have adventures, to try new foods, to buy new products and to see how other people live. Tourism is the largest industry in the world because it plays an important role in our lives – providing us with opportunities to expand our horizons and broaden our perspectives. This is why it has been an important factor in every society for countless centuries. People are naturally curious and feel a need to satisfy their curiosities about the many different ways in which people have organized their cultures and developed their societies.

In his book, *The Art of Travel*, Alain de Botton offers an insight into the way our travels relate to our desire to gain insights into our lives. He writes:

> If our lives are dominated by a search for happiness, then perhaps few activities reveal as much about the dynamics of this quest – in

all its ardor and paradoxes – than our travels. They express, however inarticulately, an understanding of what life might be about, outside of the constraints of work and of the struggle for survival. (Botton, 2002: 9)

Our travels, then, must be seen as having a more profound significance than we might imagine and de Botton's insight helps us gain a different perspective on the importance of travel for people.

I've never been to Japan, but its culture strikes me as not particularly tourist-friendly. It's still a pretty rigid, formalistic, dense society, and those factors make it less accessible to Auslanders than some others. Further, there's an element of xenophobia that's inherent in Japanese culture, whether still overt or not, that makes that inaccessibility border on the hostile. I'm not criticizing, by the way. I don't see anything inherently wrong with most of that (unless it devolves into militant Emperor worship, and history has shown that that circumstance has some unpleasant side effects), but it does mean that Japan will never be a great location for a lot of types of vacation outside of more adventurous visitors. I say all that as an American/Westerner. (Gen. Kanai weblog: Tourism in Japan.)

A visit to Japan is usually filled with anxiety and excitement. There is a strangeness to the place; it seems different, chaotic – yet exotic. Major cities such as Tokyo or Osaka seem confused – and confusing – and the first time visitor feels lost. Unlike the American city, Japan offers few gridiron street plans with the convenient 'A' Streets and First Avenues. Nor is there a comprehensible centralized urban pattern like that of the medieval European town. Even products in stores look different. The people are different in their form, manners, and dress. Most of all, the language is different, beyond comprehension – strange in its sound and more so in its written form. The city seems filled with meaningless marks, however pretty or intriguing their pattern. (Treib & Herman, 1993: viii)

Chapter 2

Japan and the Tourism Industry

In this chapter I will offer some statistics about tourism as a worldwide phenomenon, with a focus on tourism in Japan. As I pointed out earlier, tourism is the largest industry in the world and in 2006 there were approximately 900 million international visits by tourists. Some of these visits are by tourists in countries that are next to one another or very near to one another, so the figures on international visits do not tell us the whole story, but they do give us a good idea of the size of the industry. Countless other millions of tourists visited sites in their own country.

Statistics on World Tourism

Although Japan is an industrial giant, and has a rich and fascinating culture, it is not a major tourist destination. But it is developing its tourism industry as shown in Table 2.1. It is useful to know where foreign tourists, who visit Japan, come from. Table 2.2 is drawn from the Japan Association of Travel Agents and lists the top visitors to Japan by nationality for 2002. We can see that most of the foreign visitors to Japan come from Asian countries, with the exception of tourists from the United States. There are a large number of Japanese living in the United States and a number of these visits may be from Japanese, who are returning home for one reason or another. These countries are the only ones that sent more than 100,000 visitors to Japan. Quite likely, a number of these visits were not made by tourists but by people doing business with Japanese companies. Since tourism has greatly increased in Japan in recent years, these figures considerably underestimate the number of visitors to Japan in 2007.

These tables reveal that most visitors to Japan come from the neighbouring countries of Japan – Korea, Taiwan, China, Hong Kong and the Philippines.

Table 2.1 Growth of international tourism in Japan

Year	1990	1995	2000	2004
Foreign arrivals	3,226,000	3,345,000	4,527,000	6,138,000

Table 2.2 Visitors to Japan by nationality in 2003

Country	*Number of visitors*
Korea	1.2 million
Taiwan	877,000
USA	731,000
China	452,000
United Kingdom	219,000
Hong Kong	136,000
Canada	131,000
Philippines	129,000
Germany	93,000
France	87,000
Singapore	76,000
Thailand	72,000

The United States is the only exception, sending 731,000 visitors to Japan.

Germany only sent 93,000 visitors to Japan in 2003 and France only sent 87,000 visitors – which is interesting because Germany is second and France is third in terms of per capita expenses for tourism and they both provide their workers with an excess of 20 vacation days per year.

In 2004, Japan had around 6 million international visitors but about 23 million Japanese travelled abroad; a tourism imbalance of more than three to one. The JNTO, as I mentioned earlier, hopes to have 10 million international tourists by 2010, and is waging an aggressive advertising campaign to do so. Unfortunately, because of the worldwide economic downturn in 2009, it is unlikely that Japan will get 10 million international tourists by 2010. To understand where Japan ranks in terms of international tourist arrivals in general, consider the chart on the world's most important tourist destinations. It is derived from the United Nations World Tourist

Organization (the *World Tourism Barometer*, Vol. 5, No. 2) and offers international arrivals in millions of visitors. I have rounded off the population figures in Table 2.3. It is instructive to see which countries spend the most money on tourism. Table 2.4 lists the five countries that spend the most money on tourism.

The website of the World Tourist Organization lists the top tourism spenders as the United Kingdom, Germany, France, Japan and the United States. Table 2.5 shows their expenses, the size of their populations and their per capita expenditures on tourism for 2005. This material was supplied by the United Nations World Tourism Organization (UNWTO).

Table 2.3 Most popular international tourism destinations in 2007

Country	2007 visitors (million)	Population
France	81.9	64 million
Spain	59.2	40 million
USA	56	300 million
China	54.7	1.3 billion
Italy	43.7	57 million
United Kingdom	30.7	58 million
Germany	24.4	82 million
Ukraine	23.1	46 million
Turkey	22.2	71 million
Mexico	21.4	109 million

Table 2.4 Expenditures on tourism by countries in 2005

Country	Billions of USD
United States	99.6
Germany	80.2
United Kingdom	73.7
Japan	48.1
Italy	26

Source: www. Nationmaster.com

Table 2.5 Per capita expenses on tourism in 2005

Country	United Kingdom	Germany	France	Japan	United States
Expenditure	59.6	72.8 billion	31.2 billion	37.5 billion	69.2 billion
Population	60 million	82 million	61 million	127 million	300 million
Per capita ($)	987	882	514	295	234
Ranking	1	2	3	4	5

This table shows that Japan comes in at the fourth position in terms of per capita expenditures on international tourism, so the Japanese travel to other countries in considerable numbers but other countries do not travel to Japan in great numbers. There is a correlation between the wealth of countries and international tourism. The countries with the largest per capita expenditures on tourism are also among the wealthiest countries in the world.

There is a correlation between the average number of vacation days in a country and tourism expenditures except for the United States. Table 2.6 lists the average number of vacations days by country and their ranking by per capita tourism expenditures.

Americans who travel abroad frequently can make arrangements to use stored-up vacation time so that they can have more time on their trips, but obviously it is much easier for citizens of the countries with the most vacation days to travel for extended periods of time.

The statistics on world tourism show that Europe is the major tourist destination for tourists, with Asian and Pacific nations far below Europe. Table 2.7 shows international tourism by regions. The data were supplied by the UNWTO.

Table 2.6 Average number of vacation days by country

Days	Country	Ranking on tourism expenditures
37	France	3
35	Germany	2
28	United Kingdom	1
25	Japan	4
13	USA	5

Table 2.7 International tourism by regional market share

Europe	*Asia*	*Americas*
54.5%	20%	16.5%

Obviously, Asian and Pacific countries have a great deal of work to do if they are to catch up to Western Europe, including Southern and Mediterranean Europe. Approximately 400 million international visits were for recreation and leisure and about 120 million visits were for business or attending conventions. Finally, 185 million visits were to visit friends and relatives and for medical tourism purposes. In many cases, international visitors combined recreation and business.

It is instructive to look at the international destinations of American tourists. In 2004, more than 27 million Americans travelled abroad, with large number of them going to European countries. In Table 2.8, I list the major destinations in terms of the numbers of Americans who visited each country. These data were supplied by the Office of Travel and Tourism Industries (OTTI) for 2004. In 2004, more than 60 million United States residents travelled abroad.

These figures show that Japan ranks ninth in terms of foreign countries that Americans visit, ahead of Taiwan, Australia, Spain, Ireland, India and Greece. The number of tourists from the United States increased considerably from the figures from 2003 (if the figures are accurate). So

Table 2.8 Major foreign destinations of American tourists in 2004

Mexico	19,360,000
Canada	15,056,000
United Kingdom	3,692,000
France	2,407,000
Italy	1,915,000
China	1,805,000
PRC	1,067,000
Hong Kong	738,000
Germany	1,750,000
Jamaica	1,258,000
Japan	1,067,000

although Japan lags behind other Asian countries in terms of total number of foreign tourists, it is doing tolerably well as far as attracting people living in America for visits, either for family reasons, recreational purposes, business meetings or conventions – and in many cases, combinations of these reasons.

What Americans Do When They Visit Japan

Thanks to an in-flight survey sponsored by the United States Department of Commerce, we have a pretty good idea what US travellers do when they visit Japan. This material comes from a survey of air travellers conducted between January and December 2005, as shown in Table 2.9.

This table suggests that tourists who visit Japan are primarily interested in Japanese culture and society in contrast to activities such as gambling (1.3%), attending sporting events (4.4%) or going on environmental/eco excursions (2.2%). Tourists generally are interested in sampling foreign cuisines, which is an important way of experiencing a different culture. This explains why dining is at the top of the list for Japan. It is at the top of the list for Western European countries and most of the other countries that Americans visited. There are 'gourmet tours'

Table 2.9 Favourite activities of US travellers in Japan (in percentages)

Dining in restaurants	86
Shopping	80
Visit historical places	48
Sightseeing in cities	41
Cultural heritage sites visited	34
Visit small towns	30
Tour countryside	23
Visit art galleries, museums	18
Night clubs, dancing	15
Guided tours	14
Amusement/theme parks	14
Ethnic heritage sites	14
National parks	9

Note: I have rounded off the figures for this chart.

in many countries for tourists who are particularly interested in fine dining experiences.

Shopping is another important activity for tourists, who want to bring back souvenirs of the places they have visited or take advantage of bargains when that is possible. Most of the remaining items on the list involve seeing what is distinctive about Japanese culture: visiting cultural heritage sites, sightseeing in cities and then visiting small towns (where a different kind of Japan from huge cities like Tokyo can be experienced).

Activities of Japanese Tourists in Foreign Countries

It is instructive to examine the activities of Japanese tourists in foreign countries. A survey of Japanese tourists to Copenhagen in 2002–2003 offers us some insights into how they spend their time. A good deal depends on whether the tourists are in groups or are on their own, and the data do not reveal details on this matter. Also, the cities or countries where we find tourists affect their behaviour and the way they allocate their time. So the data on Copenhagen have to be seen in terms of what Copenhagen and Denmark have to offer tourists. These statistics for Japanese tourists in Copenhagen are shown in Table 2.10.

Table 2.10 Activities of Japanese tourists in Copenhagen

Visit attractions, sights	22.4%
Visit museums	13.3%
Go to theatre	1.1%
Go to concerts, festivals	2.3%
Walk around town	17.4%
Organized sightseeing tour	6.0%
Go out at night	2.1%
Shopping	13.9%
Dine in restaurants	7.5%
Attend sports event	0.6%
Participate in sports event	0.3%
Attend a Congress	1.8%
Business meetings	2.4%
Excursion outside city	6.4%
Other	2.6%

While it is impossible to generalize about the behaviour of Japanese tourists in all foreign countries, it is reasonable to assume that these figures are indicative of the way in which Japanese tourists spend their time when visiting foreign countries. When Japanese tourists are in group tours, there may be considerable differences in the way they allocate their time since the tour shapes a tourist's experience in a foreign city or country. The following discussion of typical Japanese group tours demonstrates this.

Japanese Tourists in Bali

Shinji Yamashita, a Japanese tourism scholar, describes the 'typical' Japanese tourist visit to Bali, in his book *Bali and Beyond*. Bali is a 10-hour flight from Japan and thus easily accessible to Japanese tourists. These tourists, he says, often come on short five-day group package tours that follow this schedule:

Day 1: They arrive in late afternoon or evening and settle in.

Day 2: They go sightseeing, buy souvenirs and attend a Barong dance.

Day 3: They visit various craft villages such as Celuk or Mas or Ubud. That evening they generally watch a kecak 'monkey' dance and have a lobster dinner

Day 4: They fly to Yogyakarta to visit the temple at Borodudur and return to Bali that evening.

Day 5: They wander around shopping – they buy souvenirs and then take an evening flight back to Japan.

Japanese tourists on these package tours are very busy, then, and are usually away from their hotels all day long – from early in the morning until late in the evening. This means they do not get to enjoy the views of the sea from the hotel rooms they have booked. Yamashita suggests that touring is seen as a kind of 'work' for Japanese travellers, who become upset if they miss something important. Westerners, who generally come for stays of one or two weeks, are usually much more relaxed about their sightseeing and shopping.

He offers an interesting statistic: Japanese tourists account for 20% of the tourists in Bali but they spend 50% of the money spent on souvenirs there. They devote a much higher percentage of their time shopping than do tourists from western countries, and are particularly interested in purchasing branded items. One reason for this is the fact that Bali is very cheap for Japanese tourists and Japan is a gift-giving and gift-receiving culture.

Conclusions

These statistics provide us with an overview of the tourism industry and offer insights into the way tourists typically spend their time. When tourists visit foreign countries, they generally want to learn something about the cultures they are visiting and they do this by sampling the food, purchasing souvenirs and seeing important sights. There are different kinds of tourists – some people like to wander around on their own while others prefer package tours, which promise them an easier trip, guides to point out matters of importance and in some cases a comprehensive picture of the country or countries being visited.

The discussion of Japanese tourists in Bali suggests that they tend to be 'driven' and work very hard to make certain that they do not miss any important site or experience. One reason for this may be because on a short five-day stay in Bali, there is so much to see and do that Japanese tourists on these short package tours are forced to work very hard to take in everything, to see everything and to photograph everything. They are not different from tourists from other countries in these regards, but their limited time period makes their vacations in Bali highly pressurized.

Frommer's Travel Talk: Japan

- *Independent travel Honshu-Hokkaido (2 messages, 2 new)*
- *Hankyu International Hotel Osaka (1 message, 1 new)*
- *Japan Rail Pass (5 messages, 2 new)*
- *Learning Japanese (7 messages, 1 new)*
- *Rail passes (6 messages, 1 new)*
- *Tickets to sumo in Tokyo May 2007 (1 message, 1 new)*
- *How crowded 3R trains 15–26 May? (3 messages)*
- *Mitsukoshi warning (1 message)*
- *Souvenirs in Japan (2 messages)*
- *Hakone – how easy is it? (8 messages)*
- *Where to stay in Koyasan, Japan? (5 messages)*
- *Nikko or Kamakura? (6 messages)*
- *Is sushi safe everywhere in Japan? (3 messages)*
- *Go to Japan in July? (new)*
- *Independent travel (2 messages)*
- *What is Sendai like? (2 messages)*
- *Free tour guides in Kyoto (3 messages)*
- *Simple phrase book (new)*
- *Takayama accommodation and things to see (3 messages)*
- *First items on Travel Talk Page for Japan on Frommer's website (as of 3 May 2007)*

Chapter 3
Japan on the Internet

When tourists think about visiting a foreign country, one of the first things many of them do is look up that country on the internet. After they have narrowed their choices down to one or two countries, they often purchase guidebooks to these countries to get a better idea of what they offer and what a trip in that country will cost.

Googling Japan

If you type questions relating to tourism in Japan into Google, you get the following number of sites (accessed 7 March 2009):

Topic	*Websites*
Japan tourism	8,780,000
Japan tours	6,670,000
Japan travel	65,700,000
Japan package tours	827,000
Japanese culture	31,200,000

So anyone contemplating a visit to Japan can find a mind-boggling number of sources that deal with what Japan has to offer tourists and information about tours, travel arrangements and other matters of interest.

There are some websites run by publishers of travel guides that are full of information. One of the most popular is Frommer's 'Travel Talk'. If you

Table 3.1 Asian countries on Frommer's Travel Talk

Country	Discussions	Posts
China	868	4799
India	335	1536
Japan	800	3658
Thailand	872	3593
Vietnam	411	1832

go to Asia on the 'Travel Talk' website, you find discussions and posts for the following countries, which I have selected from the total list on the site on the day I accessed it (8 March 2009).

We can see from Table 3.1 that Japan ranks third in terms of number of discussions found on a website, just behind China and well ahead of India and Vietnam. Thailand had around 12 million foreign tourists in 2006, so the number of inquiries relative to the number of foreign tourists is small. All of these countries are trying to increase the number of foreign tourists visiting them because of the financial benefits that tourism brings.

Thanks to the internet, tourists contemplating a visit to Japan can find an enormous amount of material about the country from a variety of sources: the JNTO, websites listed on Google, blogs and sites such as Frommer's 'Travel Talk', which has a site for people to make comments and ask questions about many different countries. The Lonely Planet website also has a place where people can ask questions about countries they plan on visiting and others will answer their questions and send in comments about their trips to that country.

As you can see from the material on 'Travel Talk: Japan' at the beginning of this chapter, most of the questions have to do with transportation, housing and food, which is only logical. Some people wanted to find out about online travel agents while others asked about whether they should go to one city or another one. Tourists contemplating a visit to a different country generally want to find out about these matters. The question that got the most answers on the first pages of the site involved one from the mother of a 6-month-old baby, who asked whether she could cope with Japan with her baby. There were 21 responses to this enquiry.

'Japan Tourism' on Google

If you were to type 'Japan Tourism' into Google, you would find that there are 8,780,000 websites for this topic. The first five sites you get are listed below (for 8 March 2009, when I accessed the website):

- *Japan National Tourist Organization website*
  Japanese government site providing information for online budget Reservations, regional guides ...
- *Japan National Tourist Organization*
  Special attractions, World Heritages in Japan, An Invitation 'Otaku' tour ...
- *Official Tourism Guide for Japan Travel*
  Yokoso Japan. A complete guide to Japan ...
- *Japan Travel Guide*
  Association for independent tourism assistance in Japan ... Free guide/Interpreter service. ...
- *Tourism in Japan – Wikipedia, the free encyclopedia*
  Jan. 15, 2009. Following the Meiji Restoration and the building of a national railroad network.... .

We can see, then, that the JNTO website has a commanding position on the web for anyone who typed 'Japan Tourism' into Google. This website has an enormous amount of material on every aspect of tourism in Japan and provides people with information about hotels, restaurants, sites of importance and Japanese culture.

The first two sponsored links (advertisements) on the right had side of the page listing the unsponsored links were as follows:

- *Japan tourism*
  Call and speak to our experts ...
  and
- *Vacation deals*
  Great vacation rates

It is quite likely nowadays that people contemplating touring Japan will consult the internet to investigate travel opportunities there. It is now possible to book rooms in hotels, obtain tickets for musical, theatrical and other performances, and make other travel arrangements using the internet.

The responses to Japan Tours were quite different from the ones for Japan Tourism. There were about 6,670,000 responses to Japan Tours and most of them were 'sponsored links', which is the Google way of saying 'advertisements'. On the first page of this site there were many 'sponsored links' from companies such as Affordable Tours, Adventures Abroad and Travelocity. This topic, 'Japan Tours', is different from 'Japanese Tourism' in that 'Japan Tours' suggests that a person is looking for a company to book a tour with, whereas 'Japanese Tourism' suggests that a person is interested in the subject of visiting Japan but not ready to make a commitment and book a tour to Japan.

Nowadays, anyone planning a trip to any country should investigate that country, its attractions, scams in it to beware of and related matters on the internet at sites such as 'Travel Talk', 'The Thorn Tree', Virtual Tourist, TripAdvisor, blogs and other sites that will contain information on such things as hotels, restaurants and places to visit or avoid.

Japan on YouTube

There are a large number of videos, of varying quality, about Japan on YouTube, and tourists interested in seeing videos about various aspects of Japanese culture and society can get some useful insights by going to this site and typing in topics such as 'Japanese fast foods', 'Sumo wrestling', 'Japanese convenience stores', 'Japanese temples and shrines' and any other topic of interest. You will be able to watch videos of varying lengths – from 15 or 20 seconds to 8 or 9 minutes about Japanese culture. I have posted half a dozen short videos that I took on my most recent trip to Japan on YouTube. You can find them by typing in 'decoderman'.

Conclusions

It is very useful for travellers planning to visit Japan to read some guidebooks on Japan and to search on the internet for information about hotels, restaurants, places to visit and other matters relating to tourism. I was able to find a moderately priced room in Takayama by using the Rakuten website (which advertises itself as 'Japan's Number 1 Hotel Booking Site') and I got my airline tickets from Sankei Travel in San Francisco, which is a branch of a company in Japan. Their e-mail address is info info@sankeisanfrancisco.com. The agent I dealt with there was very helpful with other matters as well. The JNTO's website www.jnto.com is also full of valuable information.

I was able to make reservations for hotels in Takayama and Kyoto using the internet and e-mail with little difficulty. I wanted to stay at Toyoko business hotels in Tokyo and Kanazawa, but when I tried to use the Toyoko internet site, I found it was impossible to use for someone who does not know Japanese. So I called several hotels (the addresses and phone numbers of all Toyoko hotels are listed on the company's website) and I discovered that nobody at these hotels spoke English. The only English word the women who answered the phones at the hotels I called knew was 'sorry'. And there was not an e-mail site I could use.

I did find a phone number for the business office of the Toyoko chain and called that number. I found a very helpful woman there who spoke halting English and finally was able to make my reservations, but it was quite an ordeal obtaining those reservations – in part, because the woman who answered the phone did not speak English very well. It turned into high comedy when I tried to give her my e-mail address, since she did not recognize some letters and I speak with a Bostonian's accent.

The Toyoko chain has 200 hotels, all over Japan, and a room for two people in these hotels costs around 8100 yen, or approximately $80, that is depending on the price of yen. You have to wait until 4:00 PM to get your room at Toyoko hotels but you can leave your suitcases with the hotel if you come earlier. I booked a room at one of the two Toyoko hotels in the Asakusa (pronounced 'asaksa') section of Tokyo, so we could see the Sanja Matasuri, a huge and very exciting religious festival that takes place there on the third Sunday in May. It is, so I understand, the largest and wildest festival in Tokyo and got our trip to Japan off to a memorable beginning.

Part 2
Semiotic Japan

Perhaps the most influential post-Second World War book on semiotics was Barthes' Elements of Semiology. *In this elaboration of Saussure, Barthes developed an extremely influential theory of the sign. According to Barthes, a sign, as articulated by Saussure, is principally a form of denotation. That is, the signifier names directly a particular object or marks out plainly to what it is referring. In addition, however, signs can also refer to culturally determined implications or connotations which have additional meanings. Thus, the word 'axe' denotes a particular tool for chopping wood. The possession of an axe in some cultures, however, may also connote a high social status.* (Gottdiener, 1995: 15)

What is to be learned from the simple historical fact that the great-grandparents of many Japanese alive today had no names? Seeing Japan as a group society, we conclude that there was no notion of individuality among the Japanese until a few generations before our own. No individuality, and for the vast majority no history – just as the serfs of feudal Europe lived out lives as unrecorded as the lives of farm animals. (Smith, 1997: 42)

Karasu ni bampo no kō ari.

The filial duty of feeding one's parents is known even to the crow. (Hearn, 1967)

Chapter 4
Semiotic Japan

Introduction

In this section I use a variety of disciplines such as semiotics, psycho-analytic theory, sociological theory and other methodologies that are commonly used in a multi-disciplinary approach to media and cultural phenomena known as cultural criticism. This approach enables us to understand those iconic aspects of Japanese culture with which tourists most commonly come into contact as they travel through the country. This analysis, as I pointed out earlier, is modelled upon the kind of semiotic interpretation of Japanese culture found in Roland Barthes' seminal book on Japan, *Empire of Signs*. The topics I deal with are signs and what I attempt to do is explain their relationship to covert Japanese cultural codes, their various connotations and their psycho-socio-cultural significance.

A Brief Note on Semiotic Theory

When Roland Barthes titled his book on Japan *Empire of Signs*, he was announcing that he was offering a semiotic interpretation of certain aspects of Japanese culture that manifested themselves as signs. Semiotics is the science of signs, and signs can be defined as anything that can stand for something else. Words are the most commonly used signs, but so are facial expressions, hair styles, clothing, foods, objects and just about everything else. There are two founding fathers of the science, the Swiss linguist Ferdinand de Saussure, who called the science of signs *semiology* (literally words about signs) and the American philosopher Charles Sanders Peirce, who used the term *semiotics*, which is the term most favoured by semiotic scholars.

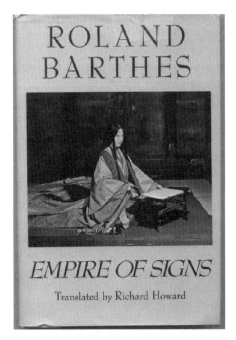

Cover of Roland Barthes' *Empire of Signs*

In his book, *Course in General Linguistics*, Saussure explained that signs are made of two elements: a sound-image (such as a word) and a concept for which the sound-image stands. As he wrote:

> I call the combination of a concept and a sound-image a *sign*, but in current usage the term generally designates only a sound-image, a word used for example (*arbor*, etc.). One tends to forget that *arbor* is called a sign only because it carries the concept 'tree', with the result that the idea of the sensory part implies the idea of the whole.

> Ambiguity would disappear if the three notions here were designated by three names, each suggesting and opposing the others. I propose to retain the word sign (signe) to designate the whole and to replace *concept* and *sound-image* respectively by *signified* (*signifié*) and *signifier* (*signifiant*); the last two terms have the advantage of indicating the opposition which separates them from each other and from the whole of which they are part. (Saussure, 1966: 67)

What is important to recognize, Saussure added, is that the relationship between the signifier and signified is arbitrary, based on convention.

What semioticians do when they are adopting a Saussurean approach, is to examine signifiers and try to discern or interpret what is signified by them, in the broadest sense of the term.

The other approach, by Peirce, suggests that there are three kinds of signs. As he wrote:

> Every sign is determined by its object, either first, by partaking in the character of the object, when I call the sign an *Icon*; secondly, by being really and in its individual existence connected with the individual object, when I call the sign an *Index*; thirdly, by more or less approximate certainty that it will be interpreted as denoting the object, in consequence of a habit (which term I use as including a natural disposition) when I call the sign a *Symbol*. (quoted in J. Jay Zeman, 'Peirce's Theory of Signs' in T. Sebeok, *A Perfusion of Signs*, 1977: 36)

Icons signify by resemblance (e.g. a photograph of a person), Indexes signify by causal connection (e.g. smoke signifies fire) and symbols by convention (e.g. words and gestures) which must be learned. My own inclination is to use both approaches to signs, although in practice I find Saussure's methodology most useful. When semioticians examine a country such as Japan, they look for signs (or, more precisely signifiers) that reveal important things about the culture (the hidden signifieds), which explains why Barthes' *Empire of Signs* is so fascinating, for he offers, in the topics he deals with, all kinds of remarkable insights and revelations.

One problem semioticians face is that signs can lie; for example, brunettes who dye their hair blonde are, semiotically speaking, lying with signs. In many countries, it is hard to determine whether a blonde woman is really a blonde or someone who had dyed her hair blonde; in Japan, when you see a blonde Japanese woman, you know that she has dyed her hair blonde, so dying one's hair blonde in Japan has a different meaning from dying one's hair blonde in a country where there are natural blondes and where it is difficult to know whether a blonde woman (or man) is a natural blonde. In contemporary Japan, many Japanese men and women have red tints in their hair and some Japanese young people dye their hair red, orange and other bright colours.

Often signs exist within other larger signs or sign systems, and sometimes no sign (no response to a question, for instance) is also a sign. Thus, if we are considering sumo wrestling as an important sign of Japanese culture, we can think of these wrestlers as conveying many signs such as the way their hair is tied in topknots, their physical size, the aprons they wear (mawashi), the ring where the matches take place (dohyo), the rituals involved in the sport such as throwing salt and stamping their feet, the Shinto-like costumes of the referee (gyoji) and the facial expressions of the wrestlers. We might also consider the quality of the lighting in the ring and the reactions of the audience to the match. So signs can be quite complicated and difficult to interpret, especially since the relation among the elements of signs, signifiers and signifieds is arbitrary and based on convention.

Codes

Cultures can be thought of being composed of a wide variety of codes or ways of behaving, rules that are passed on from generation to generation, that affect human relationships. They are directives, often quite specific, that often function below our level of awareness. The codes that I find most interesting are those which deal with relationships among people and aesthetic codes, which involve the arts and design.

As an example of the way in which codes shape behaviour, consider the Japanese house and the way in which the Japanese people relate to their homes explains why the code of 'perfection' is necessary in Japan – it is required because of the burden of its population. Clotaire Rapaille writes:

> Their country comprises only 146,000 square miles (compared to more than 3.2 million square miles in the United States). There was never a vast frontier to explore. The Japanese couldn't 'dispose' of their houses or their property if they grew disenchanted; they needed to make the most of their land and keep it as productive as possible. In addition, because so many people live in such a small space (the population of Japan is more than 125 million; that's 43 percent of the American population in 4 percent of the space), efficiency is critical. There's no room for wasted products or wasted process. Mistakes are costlier. Quality is a necessity. 'Perfection is a premium'. (Rapaille, 2006: 136)

We can understand, then, how the size of the population of Japan has forced the Japanese to find ways to live with large numbers of other people. Rapaille discusses how rooms in Japanese homes have multiple functions and adds that in Japanese there is no word for intimacy. Intimacy is not possible, he says, when people live in very close quarters and have no privacy.

A Japanese cultural anthropologist Mizuko Ito (in an e-mail to futurologist Howard Rheingold on 14 January 2002) offers a personal perspective on the pressure Japanese face because of their small homes. She writes:

> Things that many middle class urban Americans have that most middle class urban Japanese don't have include homes large enough to entertain friends and colleagues, private bedrooms for children, kitchens

with storage space and appliances, more than one car, extra parking space at home, free parking for cars when out, cheap gas, toll free expressways, PC with internet access (and space to put a PC in the home), more than one phone line with competitive phone rates (this just recently changed in Japan).

All these items work for the use of private and against the use of street and public spaces. Americans move between nucleated homes, private transport and often private offices and cubicles as well, with quick forays in the car to shop occasionally (not daily grocery shopping as in Japan), and use of public space and restaurants has the sense of an optional excursion rather than a necessity. In Japan most people have to meet people outside the home. In Tokyo, I find myself occupying more quasi-public spaces conducive to texting because car usage is prohibitively expensive, my home is small, and it takes a long time on foot and public transport to get anywhere. (quoted in Rheingold, *Smart Mobs*, 2003: 23)

Rheingold explains in his book that he had his 'epiphany' about the importance of cell phones and the development of what he calls 'smart mobs' when he noticed that people on the streets in Shibuya were not talking on their cell phones but staring at them and sending text messages. It was in Japan that Rheingold got the insight that led him to write the book. We can see, then, that the pressure of population and the limited amount of personal space available to the average Japanese person, even to relatively affluent professors, has an impact on everything from shopping to socializing.

I begin my semiotic analysis of Japanese culture with one of its most distinctive aspects, one that is highly structured (or 'coded') and one of the most dominant and universally recognized signs of Japanese culture, sumo wrestlers. After my analysis of sumo wrestling, I will deal with other 'iconic' aspects of Japanese culture and society such as the Japanese flag, Japanese school children (in their uniforms), Japanese baseball, Zen rock gardens, geishas, the Sanja Matsuri festival in Asakusa, department stores, manga and the Tokyo subway system map.

Sumo Wrestlers

The sumo wrestler is one of the most widely known icons of Japanese culture. Most people who travel to Japan know about sumo wrestlers; even if they do not attend a match that they have probably seen something about sumo wrestlers in newspapers and travel guides and possibly seen sumo wrestlers on television – either on programmes showing a match or on television commercials featuring them. Japan has the distinction of being the only country where there are professional sumo wrestlers and the stables that develop them.

Sumo wrestling has a long history in Japan, dating back for several thousand years. Until recent decades there was a kind of racial purity to sumo, as only Japanese men were sumo wrestlers. But now wrestlers from Korea, Hawaii, Mongolia and other countries have become sumo wrestlers, and what is even worse for the national psyche, foreign sumo wrestlers have become *yokozunas* or grand champions. One Korean sumo wrestler, Rikidozan, abandoned sumo and became a professional wrestler in 1951, giving professional wrestling some notoriety. He was proclaimed World Champion in 1954 (one of any number of world champions in professional wrestling) and was stabbed and died in 1963 in a cabaret in Akasaka, Tokyo.

In 1967, the first person who was not an Asian – a Hawaiian – reached the top ranks and since then there have been a number of men from Hawaii,

Fans turn up in hordes to watch the top sumo wrestlers clashing
Source: © Lucy Corne

Samoa, Bulgaria and even Mongolia who have become sumo wrestlers. So in the past 50 years or so, sumo has been internationalized and in the eyes of many Japanese, it has lost its special Japanese character. This internationalization of sumo goes against the grain of Japanese culture, which divides the world into two spheres: that which is Japanese and everyone and everything else.

The matches themselves are very short, often lasting only 10 or 15 seconds. In unusual matches, they might last a minute. The goal of the match is to force an opponent out of the ring or have part of his body, other than the soles of his feet, touch the ring. The contest is preceded by a ritual that lasts for a few minutes, as the wrestlers purify the ring in which they will wrestle by throwing salt on it and they perform certain exercises, like stamping their feet. Until sumo modernized itself, to suit television among other things, wrestlers could take as much time as they wanted in their pre-match rituals. This indefinite period was shortened to four minutes to suit the taste of fans and of the television networks.

Sumo wrestlers wear their hair in topknots, and wear a silk belt, a *mawashi*, which looks like a glorified diaper. These wrestlers can be classified, physically speaking, as morbidly obese persons, who start as normal looking persons but due to their regimen in their training camps, analogous to fattening cattle at feed lots, they become very fat. As a result of the stress on their hearts, many sumo wrestlers die in their fifties and suffer from many of the ailments of obese people. Yet they are seen as sexually desirable by Japanese women, in part due to the hero mystique of the sumo wrestlers, their wealth and their celebrity status.

In his *Japan Journals*, Donald Richie comments in a negative way on sumo wrestlers during a visit to a 'stable' he made in May 1978:

> The men are so enormous that they are like animals – fat animals, with slabs and rolls of meat and wide, vacant faces. And they behave with the silent deference of beasts, swinging their heads ... Theirs is a world of order – the old order where differences in station are never questioned. (Richie, 2004: 160)

Richie comments that the 'stable' where the sumo wrestlers live and train reminds him of a boy's school or a military barracks. His language also suggests that these wrestlers, with their 'vacant' faces, are a bit less than human. He also discusses something important to understand about sumo wrestlers – they live by a very strict code that regulates all aspects of their behaviour when they are in their stables and their relations with one another is based on their status.

David Scott, author of *Fodor's Exploring Japan* (5th edition), offers some other insights into the sumo wrestling phenomenon:

> Sumo is Japan's national sport and an integral part of the country's cultural fabric. It can also lay strong claims to being the world's oldest sport. Its roots like in the realms of mythology, and it is said to have been popular with the gods. Before becoming a sport in the sixth century, sumo was considered to be a way of divination and a way of invoking the good will of the spirits ... Top sumo wrestlers have the status, the media attention, and riches of Hollywood stars, and are treated with the respect and deference usually only accorded to royalty. They have private fan clubs, corporate sponsors, and, it is said, the pick of Japanese women. Despite modern influences, the Shinto origins of sumo are still evident, especially in prefight rituals.

From a psychoanalytic perspective, it is possible to suggest that there is an unconscious suicidal element in men who become sumo wrestlers; they are willing to risk an early death and a lifetime of illness for short-lived fame and the possibility of riches. This unconscious death wish is probably found in all who engage in gladiatorial combats, but it is unusually strong in sumo wrestlers, who are willing to become grotesquely obese and endanger their health. The wrestlers are incredibly strong but the strain on their hearts and other physiological systems takes its toll on them as they age.

In his book, *Japan: A Reinterpretation*, Patrick Smith offers another insight into sumo wrestling, which focuses on its sacred or ritualistic aspects. He writes:

> What is sumo, the popular wrestling tradition held to extend back to 23 B.C., if not a ritual celebration of the distinction made between the included and the excluded? The two wrestlers purify the circle where they stand by dusting it with salt. They square off, squat, and stare. There is almost nothing to see, for the match usually lasts no more than a minute or two, and often mere seconds. What matters is the consequence. The sumo contest produces not so much a winner and a loser as a change in status. The vanquished is the man pushed out of the circle. (Smith, 1997: 44)

Thus, for Smith, sumo wrestling is one more example of the way the Japanese people exclude others from their culture and a wrestling match can be seen, then, as a symbolic re-enactment and reinforcing of a basic characteristic of Japanese culture – excluding foreigners from their society, to the extent that this is possible. The loser of the match becomes, if only for a moment, a foreigner. He becomes an outsider – literally if not figuratively, and the ring, the *dohyo*, the circular area in which the match is held, an area that is separated from the rest of the arena and is sanctified by the wrestlers, is, metonymically speaking, Japan.

So a sumo match is, at the unconscious level, a kind of Japanese morality play which reinforces an important aspect of Japanese culture and society – a fear of contamination by foreigners. The organization that controls sumo wrestling is attempting to stem the influx of foreigners training to be sumo wrestlers and has now issued a rule that only one foreigner can be attached to a sumo 'stable', which is where sumo wrestlers live and follow their rigorous and tradition-bound training schedule.

This matter of excluding foreigners is discussed by Hall in his book *Cartels of the Mind: Japan's Intellectual Closed Shop*. He writes:

> The truth of the matter is that the Japanese simply do not want non-Japanese physically present among them for any length of time, embedded as individuals in the working institutions of their society. As short-term feted guests or curiosities, yes; but not as fixed human furniture. Permanent intrusions are viewed by Japanese as intolerable threats to their value system, their social relationships, their way of life. (Hall, 1998: 178)

There seems to be a diminishing of interest in sumo in the younger generations of Japanese, perhaps because younger Japanese are more international in their outlook and an enactment of the ritual exclusion of others by sumo wrestlers does not interest Japanese youth. There have also been allegations that there have been fixed matches, which has shaken the somewhat sacred aura of sumo wrestling and disturbed those who follow the sport. The current champion is a Mongolian who seems to be having psychological problems and stopped wrestling for a while – he left Japan for a visit to Mongolia. We have two violations of the Japanese code here: one, a sumo champion is not Japanese (this is not new for their have been other foreigners who were champions) and two, a sumo champion leaves Japan, violating Japanese sacred space and the bond between Japanese sacred space and sumo champions.

Geishas

Geishas are, along with sumo wrestlers, one of Japan's most iconic figures and play a major role in the way Japanese culture is perceived by people all over the world. We find geishas on most travel literature because these women are supreme examples of what we might call 'Japaneseness', and play a major role in the way non-Japanese people fantasize about Japan, Japanese women and Japanese culture. Foreigners tend to see geishas as exotic and as exemplars of what we might describe as classical hyper-femininity. One reason that geishas have so much cultural resonance is because they are connected to images foreigners have of an earlier period in Japan when the old 'mythical' Japan existed. Many visitors to Japan go there in search of this period in Japan and are disappointed to find that geishas and temples and a few other remnants of early Japan only exist in pockets here and there in Japanese cities that are full of modern skyscrapers which have been described as 'concrete jungles'.

Geisha walking in parade in Asakusa

In the 1920s, there were an estimated 80,000 geishas in Tokyo and now there are probably less than 2000 there. Geishas have been replaced, in large measure, by bar girls and other kinds of nightclub entertainers. The term 'geisha' can be translated, roughly speaking, as 'an accomplished' woman. Geishas are traditionally trained to be gifted conversationalists, singers, musicians and dancers. Whether geishas usually had sexual relationships with their clients is a murky subject. There is a debate among scholars about whether geishas are prostitutes and part of the sex trade in Japan.

Are Geishas sex workers

A Japanese writer, Kanzaki Kiyoshi, argued in numerous newspaper and journal articles about the exploitation of geishas in Japan as late as the 1950s. As Caroline Norma writes about Kiyoshi (www.umpa.umjmeld. edu.au):

> His writings are almost unique in their assertion that the geisha system is part of Japan's sex industry. Kanzaki stands alone among scholars who nearly all imagine 'the Japanese geisha' to simply 'study classical Japanese music and dance, perform music and dance for parties in order to pay for their art lessons and elaborate stage presentations'. Scholars argue that women in the role of the 'geisha' serve a legitimate and historically important function in Japanese society 'enlivening … the banquets of elite business, military, and political men'.

Norma suggests that it was the enactment of anti-prostitution laws in the 1950s (although the geishas were left out of that law) and rules preventing parents from selling their daughters and requiring girls to attend school that ultimately led to the end of geisha prostitution. She argues that the geisha system lent respectability to prostitution in post-war Japan and her paper, she says, wants to overturn the 'dearly held historical picture of the geisha system as an institution of the arts'. According to Norma, apprentice geishas, maikos, only became geishas after they had been prostituted.

In earlier days, poor farmers often sold their daughters off into geisha slavery. The girls were forced to work in the homes of their geisha families until they paid off the price that was paid for them and for their expenses incurred in the homes where they lived and were trained. They studied singing, dancing, the proper way to wear kimonos, how to conduct tea ceremonies, ways to conduct conversations with their patrons, how to play musical instruments and other similar arts. In earlier times, in the period at the end of the 18th century, the geishas influenced popular styles for women. Unlike the elaborately dressed maiko, apprentice geishas, geisha style tends to be modest and relatively plain, but still elegant.

One reason for this geisha style is because Japanese government passed a law that prevented geishas from working outside restaurants and pleasure houses and preventing them from wearing elaborate costumes like those that were worn by courtesans. That explains why photographs of geishas show them in relatively simple kimonos with hair that is not full of combs, fans, jewellery and other objects.

Apprentice geishas (maiko)

Edward Seidensticker points out, in his book *Tokyo Rising: The City Since the Great Earthquake*, that the rise of the golf course led to the decline of the fancy restaurants where geishas worked. He writes:

> The popularity of golf among politicians, bureaucrats, and business-men may have something to do with the decline of another national accomplishment, that of the geisha, the 'accomplished person'. That there has been a very sad decline is undeniable. Tastes and ways of life are changing. The traditional music and dance which were the geisha's accomplishments do not interest the ruling classes as they once did, or provide the incentives they once did for a young girl to endure the severities of geisha training ... The decline of the geisha may be dated from the second postwar decade, when rapid economic growth was beginning. So it would not seem to be true, as if often averred, that the geisha was simply too expensive. It takes dozens of evenings at an expensive geisha restaurant to dissipate a sum equal to the membership fee in one of the golf clubs important people belong to. (Seidensticker, 1991: 332–333)

Seidensticker describes how the geisha quarters and geisha restaurants disappeared in Tokyo and how the relatively small numbers of geishas remaining there has aged.

We are led to conclude, then, that the geisha is now in many respects a cultural anachronism, of interest to tourists, and is similar in nature to other cultural anachronisms found in many cultures. Geishas now symbolize for foreigners, the ancient and more interesting Japan of the emperor, samurai warriors and sumo wrestlers and that Japan, the imagined Japan, the 'living museum' Japan, is the Japan that many tourists seek when they visit Japan. Stereotypes of Japan are numerous and incorrect ideas about Japanese culture, in general, and geishas, in particular persist to this day.

The exotic and the erotic

We can use the geisha figure to explore a term often used to describe Japan, 'exotic'. The Greek root of the word 'exotic' is *exotikos* – that is 'foreign'. In Greek *exo* means 'outside', but it is also commonly understood as unusual, strange, different and distant. The second part of the word, the '*tic*' in erotic, is a suffix used to create adjectives.

Tourists travel to distant lands in search of cultures that are different from their native ones in terms of the architecture, foods, clothes and costumes and culture, in general. Why spend money and endure the hardships caused by thousands of miles of travel to visit a city or a country that is similar to the one you came from. 'In language, there are only differences', wrote the Swiss linguist Saussure, whose ideas were discussed earlier. We can add to this, in tourism there are only differences, also – at least for large numbers of tourists. 'The entire mechanism of language … is based on oppositions' (1966: 121), Saussure added. We make sense of the world, Saussure argues, by seeing things in terms of their relationships with other things, and the basic relationship is that of oppositions. Because language structures the way we think, oppositions play an important role in our thinking.

In our thinking as tourists, it is the exotic, those aspects of a culture which are different from or opposite to our ordinary everyday lives, that helps us choose our destinations. We can also see the exotic in Japan as different from the everyday lifestyles in Japan. The problem people in 'exotic' countries face is that because it is the exotic that tourists seek when they visit foreign countries like Japan, the inhabitants of Japan must provide tourists with enough exotic experiences to satisfy them.

What happens in Japan, I would suggest, is that there is enough of the exotic 'traditional' Japanese culture available to foreign tourists to satisfy most of them. Thus, seeing a geisha walking in a parade in an Asakusa festival becomes exciting. To the list of exotic elements of Japanese culture of interest to tourists, we can add Japanese forts and castles, Japanese festivals, famous temples (which are islands of Japanese exotic culture) found here and there in cities, Japanese food and various Japanese cultural arts. All these phenomena help justify the term 'exotic' in describing Japanese culture – or, at least, segments of contemporary Japanese culture. Below I contrast everyday life in western countries with the exotic in Japan.

Everyday life in the West	*The exotic in Japan*
Near	Distant
The present	The past
Familiar	Strange
Modern	Traditional
The skyscraper	The temple and garden
The businessman (salaryman)	The geisha
Electronic	Mechanical
Euro-American cuisines	Ethnic cuisine
Suits, dresses, blue jeans	Robes, costumes

The Japanese are working hard to balance touristic expectations of the exotic and other tourist desires with the modernization, or perhaps hyper-modernization that dominates modern Japanese society. So there are, as so many of the tourist guides point out, two Japans: the one contemporary Japanese people live in and the exotic imagined Japan for tourists.

The list of contrasting opposite above shows how the exotic contrasts with its opposite, modern, everyday life in many western European societies and to some extent, in modern and postmodern Japan as well. It overstates some oppositions in an effort to show how, in certain ways, our experiences in exotic cultures differ from those that characterize everyday life in western societies. Let me suggest that the modern and the traditional are not always polar opposites, but the two terms are useful in that they suggest different realms found in western societies and Japan.

There is also the relationship between the exotic and the erotic to be considered. Geishas, with their painted white faces and kimonos, are exotic to western eyes, but they can also be seen, because of their well-known abilities to please men, as erotic figures. Quite possibly they generate sexual fantasies in men from foreign lands who see them and find them fascinating and wonder what it would be like to have sex with them. And, if many reports about geishas are correct, men who find them erotic and desirable, and can afford their fees, may actually have the chance to fulfil their desires. Of course some Japanese women who wear kimonos and who look like geishas to the unknowing eye are only prostitutes, so there is an element of geisha brand dilution involved with experiences with these women. They are just prostitutes who dress like and imitate geishas.

Being a geisha was a means towards social mobility for many women years ago. In his classic work, *Things Japanese*, published first in 1904, Basil Hall Chamberlain has a discussion of what he calls 'Singing-girls'. He writes:

> The charms of the Japanese singing-girl, or *geisha*, as the Japanese term her, have been dwelt on so often that we gladly leave them to her more ardent admirers. Deprived of her, Japanese social gatherings would lose much of their vivacity and pleasing unconstraint, and many a match, interesting to the gossips, would never be made; for quite a number of prominent men have shown their partiality for the fair warblers in the most practical of ways, namely by marrying them. (Chamberlain, 1905/2007)

He added that geishas were the only women in Japan who were skilled at conversing with others and this conversational ability was one of the geisha's most important skills.

The term 'exotic' is relative. For many tourists from third-world countries and other first- and second-world countries, America might seem also to be exotic. If you look at the clothes worn by different subcultures in American high schools, you find strange and unusual clothing and hair styles. Consider some of the subcultures of students in many of our high schools such as jocks, cheerleaders, surfers, preppies, skateboarders, white punks on dope, geeks, dorks, mods, aggies, metal heads (head bangers), skinheads, vatos (Latinos), flips, punks, goths, brothers (Blacks), dreds (Blacks with dreadlocks) and skaters (with in-line skates). Members of these groups often have their own ways of dressing, using body ornaments, and styling their hair, so tourists from Japan would probably find our subcultures quite exotic.

Another thing the geisha does is enable tourists to 'time travel', back to the period when geishas developed and started playing an important role entertaining wealthy businessmen and politicians. Costumes such as those worn by geishas may help generate a sense of nostalgia about the past in Japan when, so we imagine, life was different and perhaps more pleasing. As the popularity of the geisha fades, so does an important element of our image of Japan as an exotic destination.

The Geisha and the Salaryman

I suggest that the geisha and the salaryman can be seen as polar opposites. Let me spell out the differences between the two in more detail in the chart that follows, which, I admit, pushes things to extremes in places.

Geisha	*Salaryman*
Woman	Male
Pleasure	Work
Kimono	Dark business suit
Entertains	Makes money
Tradition	Modernity
Prostitute	Slave

The geisha's realm is pleasure and entertainment, whereas the salaryman's realm is work. The geisha is connected in the popular imagination with both the exotic and the erotic (and the erotic with the sensual and the sexual), whereas the salaryman is seen to be, in essence, as a drone. Both these cultural icons, the geisha and the salaryman, are fading into oblivion.

In the 5 January 2008 issue of *The Economist*, there is an article titled 'Sayonara, salaryman', which documents the extent to which the number of salarymen is decreasing. The article begins as follows:

> When they were young, they might spend the night in the office, sleeping under their desks. For years they would go out drinking with colleagues and clients, returning home sizzled at 3:00 AM before rising at dawn to head back to the office. They accepted boring jobs or postings to provincial backwaters without question. And they did it all simply because the company asked them to. The thought of finding another employer never crossed their minds.

That is how the 'salaryman' became the paragon of modern Japan, the white-collar hero who fashioned the world's second largest economy. (January 5, 2008: 68)

Economic problems have forced companies to scale back their benefits and to focus their attention on finding short-term workers.

We can see this by looking at statistics from Japan's Ministry of Internal Affairs and Communication.

Permanent workers in 1984	Around 85%
Permanent workers in 2007	Around 65%
Temporary workers in 1984	Around 18%
Temporary workers in 2007	Around 38%

The number of salarymen, that is permanent workers, has decreased by around 20%, whereas the number of temporary, part-time and contingent workers has increased by around 20%. These temporary workers make less than half as much money as permanent workers. These changes are creating enormous changes and tensions in Japanese society and with its low birth rate, Japan finds itself without enough workers. It is estimated that by 2030, there will be only two workers to support each pensioner in Japan. The Japanese fear that if they bring in large numbers of workers from foreign countries, the uniqueness, the distinctiveness, the 'Japaneseness' of their culture will be diluted and Japanese society will be transformed in unsatisfactory ways.

What unites the geisha and the salaryman, aside from the fact that the number of these two important cultural icons is waning is that the salarymen and their bosses and clients are often served by geishas (sometimes in more ways than one) when they go out drinking after work.

The Japanese Flag

The Japanese flag, depicting the rising sun, is a study in Japanese minimalism. The flag has a white background and a red circle, representing the sun, in the flag's middle. So we have just one colour: red in the flag. White can be construed as the absence of colour and the absence of others, in general. Contrast this flag with the maximalist American flag which has 50 stars on a blue background and alternating red and white stripes. The American flag is very busy while the Japanese flag is a study in simplicity. Officially the flag is named *nisshoki*, which means 'sun flag', but it is commonly known as *hinomaru* or 'sun disk'. The characters in the Japanese language for Japan mean 'sun origin', so we can see why the Japanese flag is connected to the rising sun. Its origins go far back in Japanese history; red circles were used by samurai warriors and the rising sun flag was adopted in 1870 as the country's official flag. Perhaps because of its links with Japanese militarism, it is not flown everyday on government buildings – only on public holidays. The size of the red disk in the centre of the flag is always three-fifths the length of the flag.

Symbolically, *hinomaru* can be seen as representing the relationship between Japan and the rest of the world. Japan is the island, the red circle, in the middle of a colourless void. For 400 years Japan cut itself off from the rest of the world and that period of isolation helped Japan develop and refine its distinctive aesthetic and its perspective on life and society. All that was important was in the red circle, which represents Japan, alone in the universe to the extent that this pose was tenable. Being an island nation, with a large population (although this population is rapidly decreasing because Japanese women are not bearing as many children as in earlier times), Japan developed certain techniques for organizing society, which can be seen in the number of rules and codes of behaviour that govern almost every aspect of life in Japan.

The red colour can be used to signify blood, danger, excitement and passion in many cultures. When combined with white, as in the Japanese flag, what the Japanese call *kohaku* (ko is for red and haku is for white), it suggests happiness and celebration. Red and white are also the colours used in the uniforms of shrine maidens, for engagement and wedding presents and also to signify a bond between a man's life and that of the gods, which is connected to supernationalism in Japanese politics.

The reticence of the Japanese to show their flag is a matter of some interest. It could be an example of a secretive cast of mind or of the fact that the Japanese see the flag as so important that they do not want to diminish its significance by showing it every day. It could also be that there is an element of collective shame, for human rights violations during the Second World War that is connected to the flag. It is also uncommon for the Japanese flag to be used as a decoration for clothing, the way flags are in the United States and Great Britain, since using the rising sun that way would be considered a sign of a lack of respect for the flag as a representation of Japanese culture and society.

In his book, *Learning to Bow,* Bruce Feiler explains why the Japanese flag is so problematic. He writes:

> Across Southeast Asia, the *hinomaru* flag quickly became the symbol for Japanese aggression. For centuries Japan was isolated and did not need a national emblem, but less than fifty years after hosting its first banner, the country began terrorizing its neighbors. Many Japanese feel as negative about their flag as other Asians do. Since Tokyo's defeat in the war, both the flag and the national anthem – a dreamy tribute to the emperor adopted around the same time as the flag – have been an undying source of bitter memories for some citizens ... As a result, the striking red sun on a plain white field, which the rest of the world has come to associate with Japan, has been virtually locked out of sight in the nation's schools for most of the last forty years. (Feiler, 1991: 214–215)

> Recently this mood has shifted, and the flag and the anthem have been staging somewhat of a government-sponsored comeback ... In effect, the government is not only making explicit in schools what has been implicit all along – that students must learn to bow not only to their teachers but to the state as well.

The Japanese flag is a symbol of nationalism and, many people feel that the requirement that students raise the flag and play the national anthem reflects a return to the nationalism and militarism of earlier years.

School Uniforms and Hikikomori: Japan's Hermit Youth

When you see Japanese school children, wearing their uniforms and being playful, you might think that Japan is taking good care of its youth. The statistics on the performance of Japanese teenagers on tests, given world wide, show that they are very highly rated, landing them in the top 10 countries as far as language skills and mathematics are concerned.

As the young children become teenagers, something starts to happen. It may be because of the intense pressure children in Japan feel to do well academically. It may be that certain aspects of Japanese culture become intolerable, but Japanese teenagers and 20-year-olds are a major problem for Japanese society. As David Scott explains in *Fodor's Exploring Japan* (5th edition):

> At the age of three or four, Japanese children start to attend kindergarten. The choice of a good school is crucial because, even from this early age, university entrance is the focus of a child's education, and there is intense pressure to do well. The heavy burden that is placed

Students in front of temple

on the shoulders of Japanese youth, especially on young men, of
whom most is expected, sometimes had disastrous consequences.

What this system of intense pressure leads to, for a variety of reasons
that will be discussed below, are the large numbers of school children and
young Japanese dropouts you do not see, because they are holed up in
their houses – the hikikomori. These afflicted souls have withdrawn from
society and stay in their rooms for months, sometimes for years and sometimes decades. They are sometimes described as Japan's 'lost generation',
and it is estimated that there are around 1 million hikikomori in Japan,
most of whom are males. There are some hikikomori in Taiwan and Korea,
but the number of hikikomori in these countries is relatively small.

We may ask: why did this problem arise in Japan and what is the cause
of it? There are many different explanations of why this phenomenon developed and many of them have to do with the nature of Japanese culture.
Let me suggest a number of them, all of which are related to one another.

The educational system

As Scott points out, from the moment they go to kindergarten, Japanese
youth are under great pressure to do well in school, at each level, so they
can eventually get into the major Japanese schools: Tokyo University or
Kyoto University. This is known as 'the escalator system', in which the
first school you attend has an impact on the next and so it goes up the line,

until 'examination hell' (*juken jigoku*), and the pressure students face to do well in exams that will determine which university they will attend.

In Japanese schools, students are forced to conform to many rules and do not show individuality. There is also a great deal of stratification with a rigid hierarchy of students developing, in which students who are slow or too smart often suffer from bullying – both physically and on the internet. This bullying has been identified as one of the major triggers of student withdrawal. What happens, often, is students who become hikikomori start missing classes (they become what are described as school refusers), then drop out, and then withdraw into their room. So educational pressure and the way Japanese schools operate are seen by many scholars as fundamental to the development of the hikikomori.

Around 95% of Japanese high school students have cell phones and now bullies use cell phones, e-mails, blogs and other forms of cyber bullying to attack their victims. And because Japan is a collectivist society, where great importance is placed on being a member of the group, other classmates generally do not defend those poor individuals who are the victims of bullying, in part because they fear that if they stand up for people being bullied, they will then become victims of school bullies. In the 26 March 2007 news article from the Voice of America, there was a report that as the result of bullying, five children had killed themselves since September 2007. The bullies physically attack their victims, extort money from them, force them to do certain things for them, insult them and do other things to humiliate those they do not like. One respondent told me that some bullies even determine the height of stockings for girls who are being bullied. The problem is exacerbated by the unwillingness or ineptitude of teachers, who may lecture about bullying but do little or nothing to stop it.

In Bruce Feiler's book *Learning to Bow*, which is about his experiences teaching in a Japanese school, he discusses a suicide that took place at his school the year that he was teaching there. He writes that the school master, where the suicide took place, asked one of the teachers why the child had killed himself. The teacher replied (1991: 247), 'He was a member of the basketball club … Some of the boys had been teasing him, beating him, even asking him to steal. He wanted it to end'. Feiler then discusses bullying and offers his explanation of the phenomenon:

> While it would be an exaggeration to say that Japanese students go to school in an atmosphere of violence, it is fair to say that schools generate a high level of stress in the form of pressure to conform and comply with the rules. This invisible violence in the school, like 'white

noise' in cities, lingers in the air, constantly reminding students of the threat of force that surrounds them at all times. A growing number of children, called 'school refusers', have responded by staying home. Other students take out their anxiety on one another in the form of teasing, taunting, or bullying .... The *ijime* pattern of student-on-student violence has become fairly well established. It begins with minor taunts – 'You stink', 'You're a germ', 'You don't belong in this school'. Then it moves on to petty crime – even forcing a student to steal candy from the 7-Eleven or a pack of cigarettes from a railroad station. And it often escalates the level of physical abuse – cigarette burns of the arms or punches in the head. Much of this goes unseen by the teachers, who know it exists but do not actively try to stop it. Most of the victims never speak out. Instead, they learn to live with their torture as just another price for being different from their peers. (Feiler, 1991: 246, 247)

Feiler's book offers a personal description of the strengths and many weaknesses of what can be described as a highly dysfunctional Japanese education system that is focused on teaching students to conform and be good citizens and not on their becoming rounded and happy children. In many cases, the children are tormented by *Kyōiku Mama*, 'Education Mothers', who pressure their children to do well at school.

He describes the day of a typical student, Takuya, who attended school for six-and-a-half hours, went to football practice in the afternoon for a few hours, dashed home at 6:30 pm and gulped down his dinner, went off to his cram school for two more hours, returned home at 10:00 pm, took a bath and then started doing his homework. It is obvious from Feiler's description of Takuya's schedule and his comments about the Japanese educational system that Japanese children are under great stress. [Some Japanese school children attend cram courses 5 or 6 days a week, year round and some *juku* help students get into better *juku*.]. He add that while the Japanese government is aware of these problems, it has not done anything to deal with them and things seem to be getting worse, as the hikiko-mori problem becomes more widespread.

Japanese families

Some scholars investigating this phenomenon focus on the dysfunctionality of Japanese families, where husbands work long hours and then go drinking with their colleagues, generally having little relationship with their children. Japanese children, especially those whose fathers are salarymen, are raised, to a considerable degree, without their fathers. And

Japanese children are subject to enormous pressure to 'succeed' in school and gain entrance to a major university. Not to do so is then seen as 'failure', for the son or daughter and for the parents. In addition, Japanese mothers focus too much energy and attention on their children, which leads to serious problems in the relationship between children and their parents and especially between mothers and their sons. Japanese mothers often sleep with their children for many years, which creates powerful but problematic bonds between mothers and their children. Some scholars argue that it is a failure of communication between parents and their children that is most responsible for the development of their children's withdrawals, but faulty communication is blamed for almost all the ills of societies everywhere.

When a youngster does become a hikikomori, Japanese parents often adopt a passive stance and assume it will be just temporary or they refuse to acknowledge the fact to others, lest this bring shame upon them. Thus some hikikomori often spend years in their rooms before their parents decide upon action. It would seem then that we have two problem areas, the educational system and the families, which are involved in the matter.

Japanese conformist culture

The school system and the Japanese family are affected by the culture at large, and Japanese culture is one that is based in large measure on conformity and obedience to various hidden norms that shape everyone's behaviour. The Japanese have a term, *seken*, which means society's 'hidden gaze', that the Japanese believe is focused upon them, leading to acquiescence and obeying the numerous codes in Japanese culture. Young people who, for one reason or another, cannot or do not conform to these codes, suffer from ostracism and other afflictions. Thus, some scholars maintain, it is the conformist culture in Japan that more or less creates the hikikomori. If you want to understand the reasons for the estimated million hikikomori, they argue, it is the negative and dysfunctional aspects of Japanese culture that conspire to push young people into becoming hermits – hermits living in their own families. This widespread illness is a result of dysfunctional aspects of Japanese culture, which have come to a head in modern Japan.

Psychological illness

Some scholars argue that the hikikomori are really psychologically disturbed young people who are no different from disturbed young people in other cultures. The young men and women typically suffer from agora-phobia, schizophrenia and other psychiatric ailments. In other words, the hikikomori are young people who suffer from depression or obsessive–compulsive psychological problems and they are not signifiers of a wide-spread social problem, of something wrong with Japanese society and culture. But the fact that there are so many hikikomori, around 1 million (130,000 students, according to White Paper of Ministry of Education, Sports, Science and Technology in 2003) in Japan, would suggest that while some of the withdrawers may have serious psychological prob-lems, the large-scale nature of the phenomenon and its locus in Japan sug-gests that it is Japanese society and culture and the Japanese educational system that play an important role in this matter.

Resistance to a destructive culture

One other way to look at the hikikomori is to take up the thread that starts when they refuse to go to school – and are classified as 'school refusers'. In a society that ostracizes those who refuse to conform, the hikikomori have turned the tables and ostracized their parents and Japanese society, resisting its pressures the only way they know, by with-drawing. In a way they have returned to their infantile state, when they experienced unconditional love, before they started becoming pressured by Japanese culture to perform and excel. There have been a number of cases in which Japanese children who seemed well adjusted and perfectly normal became hikikomori after they started attending cram schools. They went into their rooms and spent one or more (in some cases more than a dozen) years watching television, listening to music and surfing the internet. Some hikikomori have left their room to commit very serious crimes, so these young people are, in some cases, a danger to their parents, to Japanese society and to themselves.

Statistics reveal that those hikikomori who do return to society gener-ally do not get full-time jobs, find girl friends or lead what we would describe as normal lives. And there are large numbers of other Japanese youth, the Shinjinrui or 'new race' who have not rejected society as com-pletely as the hikikomori but who dye their hair bright colours and reject many of the rules of Japanese culture. In some cases these young people are an example of typical youthful rebelliousness but in others it is a dem-onstration that Japanese culture is beginning to have serious problems with young people.

Tourists who visit Japan may also see Otaku, young Japanese with passions for manga or anime or music or something else that occupies

their attention, but they do not see the hikikomori. What tourists experience when they visit Japan, even though they are immersed in it for a
short time, is a culture that is distinctive and unique in the world. Unless
these tourists have read articles or books about the problems of Japanese
schools, they have no idea of the pressure that the Japanese school system
puts on children or its all-too-often tragic consequences.

Japanese Baseball

Although sumo wrestling is the sport most identified with Japanese
culture – or, perhaps, with our mythical views of Japanese culture, baseball (*yakyu*) now is the most important professional sport in Japan. The
Japanese started playing baseball seriously in the 1980s, the game having
been introduced in earlier years by missionaries. An important event in
the development of baseball took place in 1934 when Babe Ruth, Lou
Gehrig and some other professional baseball players visited Japan, and
played games against teams of college players. Two years later professional
baseball started in Japan, with teams in Tokyo, Nagoya and Osaka. Over
the years a number of other teams were created, many of which changed
their names – except for the Tokyo Giants and Osaka Tigers, who have
retained their original names. As the political relationship with the United
States reached a crisis, in the years that followed, the Japanese pretended
that baseball was a Japanese game and found Japanese words to stand for
'balls, strikes' and other such terms.

In November 1944, the Japanese baseball league, called The Patriotic
Baseball association, ceased activities, but baseball returned in 1946. It was
thought by the Americans who were in charge in Japan and by Japanese
politicians after the war that baseball games would help improve the
morale of the Japanese people. According to Edward Seidensticker, whose
book *Tokyo Rising: The City Since the Great Earthquake* is the source of much
of my information on baseball, sumo and other aspects of Japanese culture, by 1949 there were enough teams for two leagues and by 1950 the
Japanese had fixed their stadiums so that they could play night baseball.
There are now two leagues with six teams in each league.

While baseball is an American game, the way the players train and the
way fans of the teams act have a distinctively Japanese flavour. Most of the
baseball stadiums are now similar in size to those in the American major
leagues, but in Japanese baseball, tie games are allowed after 12 innings.
Each of the teams all have a limit of four foreign players – two position
players and two pitchers – to prevent the game from being dominated by
players from other countries and distilling the 'Japanese-ness' of the sport.

The baseballs used in Japanese games are slightly smaller and lighter than American baseballs. At the games, fans of the home team sit in the right field bleachers and those of the opposing team in the left-hand bleachers. There are cheer leaders for the reams and the fans sing songs and make a great deal of noise.

Japanese coaches focus a great deal of attention on fundamentals of the game, such as bunting and fielding in contrast to American coaches, who stress hitting and pitching. Japanese teams are much more disciplined than American teams, which often have temperamental players involved in disputes with other players or with managers. In Japanese baseball teams, as in Japanese culture, the group/team is dominant.

What is of interest culturally speaking is the way the Japanese fans have spectacularized baseball, so that it closely resembles American football with its cheer leaders and European football with its fans of a team sitting with one another and with the singing and other partisan activities. The rule in which a game is tied after 12 innings is also very different from American baseball, where games are played until one team wins – unless the games are called because of rain or natural disasters. Games in all sports are dramatic because you never can tell what will happen and how the game will end. Allowing long games to stop, presumably because the fans would be bored or the players tired, means that some games, even if few in number, do not have a dramatic resolution or a resolution of any kind.

The most important challenge to Japanese baseball has been the flight of a number of Japanese star baseball players to American baseball teams. These Japanese players attract large numbers of Japanese-American fans and are also very popular in Japan, where American televised baseball is widely viewed. American teams, unlike Japanese teams, have no limits on the number of foreign nationals playing for a team and many American teams are full of players from various countries in the Caribbean and Latin America.

Thus the way in which baseball is played and the way in which baseball teams are manned reflects considerable differences between Japan and the United States. Japan is willing to limit the number of foreign baseball players, even though this leads to teams that are not as good as they could be with unlimited number of foreign players, whereas America accepts players from all countries and does not limit the number of foreign players on any team. A large number of foreign players on a Japanese team would alter the character of the team, since foreign players are not as willing as Japanese players to adhere to the kind of training and play demanded of Japanese players.

Rock Gardens (kare sansui)

One of the most famous iconic images of the spiritual side of Japan (as contrasted with the modern popular culture side of Japan reflected in the ubiquitous neon lights and manga) is the Zen rock garden, generally made up of rocks, pebbles and raked sand. Langdon Warner discusses the spiritual aspects of these gardens in his book *The Enduring Art of Japan*. As he explains:

> The fundamental thing about Japanese gardens, and what sets them apart from any other gardens of the civilized world, is usually lost sight of by Westerners. It is the fact that the art was definitely used in China and Japan to express the highest truths of religion and philosophy precisely as other civilizations have made use of the arts of literature and painting, of ritual dance and music. (Warner, 1952: 96–97)

Westerners, he adds, somehow vaguely recognize this matter, although they are primarily attracted by their austerity and pristine beauty.

Let me focus our attention now on the characteristics of rock gardens. According to Gouverneur Mosher, author of *Kyoto: A Contemplative Guide*, rock gardens have three characteristics: they are small, they are monochromatic and they are separated from other areas, with strong and well-delineated boundaries. They are an example of Japanese minimalism, but this minimalism has interesting psychological aspects to it, because the very simplicity of these gardens generates all kinds of different feelings in people who view them. As Mosher explains in his book:

> The origins of rock gardens seems to be clear: they appeared at a time when black-and-white painting, having been imported to Japan from China, was creating great interest, as was simultaneously the art of 'tray landscape' design. The application of these influences to garden design produced gardens in monochrome and in miniature. Because it was meant to be symbolic, a rock garden had to be small, lest its symbolism approach reality too closely and break down. Because it was small, this garden had to be clearly outlined. It was usually placed next to a building, as it tended to get lost in natural surroundings. (Mosher, 1980: 116–117)

Here, then, was a garden limited in size, colour and environment. Usually it consisted of little more that plain rocks set into a bed of white gravel. Its main virtue seemed to be permanence, for such gardens are not easily destroyed, but beyond that the limitations of the form would seem to have been too great to allow any range or depth of expression.

The truth is just the reverse. The symbolism in these gardens is sometimes nearly unlimited, for by their very simplicity and plainness, they open themselves up to an endless variety of interpretations.

Morris sees these gardens as similar in nature to modern painting. Think of abstract expressionist works that might also be limited to black and white or just a few colours. Less 'data' in abstract expressionist works generate more profound feelings and many different and in some cases conflicting interpretations.

Zen rock garden at Ryōan-ji temple in Kyoto

These rock gardens are islands of serenity set off from the chaos of modern Japanese society and reflect or mirror, it can be suggested, the Japanese sensibility of being an island nation separated from other countries, whose values and practices are thought to pose dangers to a highly distinctive Japanese culture and character. That is, they are 'islands' in Japan just as Japan is an island in the greater world, and the gardens are distinctive and quintessentially Japanese in nature. The gardens have a curious visual quality, for though they are small and confined, their spatiality conveys a sense of grandeur, representing, in many cases, islands (the rocks) in seas (the raked sand, which approximates waves). So there is an illusion of spatiality within the confines of the garden, because the scale of the rocks and sand is so perfect; the gardens are microcosms representing in a compressed scale a macrocosm, something very large – islands jutting out of huge seas.

In *A Guide to the Gardens of Kyoto*, Mark Treib and Ron Herman discuss the way these rock gardens offer respite to foreign travellers and enable them to 'time travel' and gain a sense of what Japan was like in earlier days:

> The confusion or distancing from understanding caused by the modern Japanese metropolis is less acute in historic architecture and

gardens, which are certainly more sympathetic in feeling. Quiet and repose are still found there in contrast to the density, bustle and noise of city life. In the historical gardens of Kyoto one slips back centuries to an ordered world of calm and balance. (Treib & Herman, 1980: viii)

We should be careful not to generalize too much and assume that these gardens and other refined or 'elite' aspects of Japanese culture are widely popular there, for many modern Japanese, like people in most countries nowadays, are more involved with their manga, movies, video games, cell phones and other aspects of Japanese popular culture than they are with elite Japanese culture. This elite culture or perhaps Japanese historic or traditional culture exists for some Japanese and, in large measure, for tourists. It is the distinctive and refined aesthetic sensibility of Japanese culture, as reflected in Japanese gardens, temples, forts and what we might call Japanese traditional culture that is so attractive to foreign tourists and one of the main reasons why they visit Japan. Japan, due to its island status and the fact that it was isolated for so many years, developed a distinctive culture. This culture remains here and there in Zen rock gardens, ancient forts and other old buildings, and in certain areas of cities, but like the wonderful rock gardens, it is isolated from everyday Japanese life.

Sanja Matsuri Festival in Asakusa

The Sanja Matsuri festival, held on the third Sunday and preceding Friday and Saturday of May in the Asakusa section of Tokyo, is the largest festival held in the city. I had to the good fortune to arrive in Japan the day before the festival started and to have chosen a hotel in Asakusa, which is one of the more charming parts of Tokyo. We saw the parade on Friday, the first day of the festival. It had bands, geishas and women wearing fantastic hats. I was able to take some photographs of the people marching in the parade. There must have been hundreds of thousands of people at the festival – both domestic tourists from Tokyo and other parts of the country, and international tourists. Most of the tourists attending the festival were gathered together in front of the area where the Shinto temple, so central to the festival, is located.

In this festival, teams of men and women, and in some cases only women or only children, carry elaborate *Mikashi*, shrines with deities on them. These mikashi are very heavy and sit on top and in the middle of long poles that stretch out for 15 or 20 feet in front of and behind them.

Sanja Matsuri festival in Asakusa

Sometimes it takes a team of 40 or 50 men and women to carry them, struggling as they go, through the streets. It is important to constantly jolt the *Mikashi*, so they bob up and down. This is supposed to intensify the powers of the deities that are attached to them.

During the Sanja Matsuri Festival, Asakusa becomes a huge party with Rabelaisian overtones. Different groups of carriers, each of whom have different costumes, set up tents in vacant lots and drink beer and eat in them. The hotels are all packed. We had to change our hotel room three times in four days because so many tourists and participants in the festival were in Asakusa. The ambience in Asakusa during the Festival can best be described as joyful and celebratory. This ambience suggested, to me, that there is another side to Japanese life, with all its stresses and pressures, which tourists in Japan do not recognize. Unless, that is, they are lucky enough to book a hotel in a city where a festival is being held. Festivals such as Sanja Matsuri function as a way of allowing Japanese men and women to escape from the burdens of everyday life and gain a bit of psychological release.

Mikhail Bakhtin, the Russian culture critic, explains the feeling of euphoria and oneness that crowds at festivals feel. He writes, in his masterwork *Rabelais and His World*:

> The carnivalesque crowd in the marketplace or in the streets is not merely a crowd. It is the people as a whole, but organized *in their own*

Photograph from hotel room of Sanja Matsuri festival in Asakusa

way, the way of the people. It is outside of and contrary to all existing forms of the coercive socioeconomic and political organization, which is suspended for the time of the festivity. (Bakhtin, 1984: 255)

The festive organization of the crowd must be first of all concrete and sensual. Even the pressing throng, the physical contact bodies, acquires a certain meaning. In this whole the individual feels that he is an indissoluble part of the collectivity, a member of the people's mass body. In this whole, the individual body ceases to a certain extent to be itself; it is possible, so to say, to exchange bodies, to be renewed (through change of costume and mask). At the same time the people become aware of their sensual, material bodily unity and community.

At times, after leaving the subway station in Asakusa, we had to thread our way through a sea of bodies and there was an air of excitement and joyfulness that was palpable, as crowds of people waited for the next team of Mikashi carriers to arrive. The Mikashi were carried during the day and during the evening as well, so the festival included everything from blessings by Shinto priests to late evening revelry.

In the middle ages, Bakhtin explains, the common people developed a sense of the carnivalesque to enable them to escape from the rigid morality of the church. The Sanja Matsuri festival is carnivalesque in that it is a time of pleasure, of laughter, even if it is also a festival that requires very hard work by the men and women who carry the Mikashi shrines through the streets of Asakusa. It has a religious dimension to it, but it also has a liberating, carnal, sensual aspect as well.

Women in bird hats at Sanja Matsuri festival

Authenticity and the Sanja Matsuri Festival

One reason why events such as the Sanja Matsuri festival are so popular with tourists is that they have a long history and thus are seen as authentic. This authenticity contrasts with fake staged events, called 'pseudo-events' by the American historian Daniel Boorstin, that are of dubious cultural value and are created specifically for tourists. The fact that Sanja Matsuri is religious in nature also confers on it an added value in the eyes of tourists, for religious events are seen as part of the culture and not invented to amuse tourists.

There is some question now about whether tourists, in postmodern societies such as those found in Japan and from postmodern societies such as those found in Western Europe and the United States actually care about authenticity. Erik Cohen, one of the leading sociologists of tourism, discusses the significance of authenticity in his article 'The Changing Face of Contemporary Tourism', which appeared in the July/August 2008 issue of *Society* magazine. He mentions the work of social historian Daniel Boorstin who described tourism as 'the lost art of travel' in his critique of American culture, *The Image*. This criticism, Cohen explains, was attacked by a tourism scholar named Dean MacCannell. He argued, in his highly influential book *The Tourist: A New Theory of the Leisure Class*, that tourists were seeking to escape from alienating societies in search of authenticity, but most of the time, sadly, these tourists were victimized by people in the countries they visited, who staged 'fake' tourist festivals and other similar kinds of activities.

Changes in the modern world, such as the development of postmodern societies, have made the tourist's search for authenticity more or less irrelevant and have led to the development of what Cohen calls 'the post-tourist'. He raises the question of why tourism has continued to expand. As he writes:

> One suggested explanation is that a major transformation may be underway in the West, from the modern to the post-modern tourist, or 'post-tourist'. While this is certainly not an all-embracing process, it may have wide-ranging effects on the nature of contemporary tourism. Resigned to the futility of a quest for authenticity in the contemporary world, the 'post-tourist', instead of being concerned with the origins of supposedly 'real' attractions, ironically or playfully prefers to enjoy the surfaces of often manifestly inauthentic ones. Instead of pursuing different experiences, he may choose to visit places which offer familiar ones, but in a greater variety, of a higher quality, in a more agreeable ambience (or at a lower price) than those available at home. Sheer fun and enjoyment became in this view, a culturally approved, sufficient reason for travel. (Cohen, 2008: 331–332)

I would suggest that the Sanja Matsuri festival in Asakusa attracts tourists of all kinds because it has a strong authentic pedigree and also is highly pleasing to the millions of tourists who go to see it.

The fact that large numbers of Japanese tourists come to see the processions suggests that it is not a 'fake' staged imitation of a 'real' Japanese festival. The Sanja Matsuri festival dates back to the 17th century. It is commonly described as one of the wildest and most exciting of all Japanese festivals. It offers the million or so spectators the best of two worlds: first, it is an authentic part of Japanese culture, and, second, with the drums beating and its carnivalesque atmosphere, an exciting and highly pleasurable experience for tourists and 'post-tourists'.

Manga (Japanese Comic Books)

What could be more distant from the subtle, refined, minimalist aesthetic of the Japanese rock garden than Japanese manga, the often violent and sex-crazed comic books that are so important a part of Japanese popular culture and have been so since the 1960s. Many manga show rape, incest and close ups of sexual organs of both men and women. According to Kinko Ito, a scholar of manga, in 1998, manga made up around a third of the Japanese book and magazine market. Manga are comic books that come in many different genres and appeal to various target audiences. They are created for a variety of markets such as young male and female children, male and female adolescents, older men, older women and the general public.

Ito explains that many Japanese learn to read from manga. She writes:

> Japan boasts one of the highest literacy rates in the world, even though Japanese is one of the most difficult and complicated of contemporary languages to read and write. It utilizes four different kinds of characters, two (*hiragana*) and (*katakana*) that derive from Chinese characters, *kanji* (Chinese characters), and *romanji* (Roman letters). Manga has *rubi*, or small Japanese letters written next to difficult Chinese characters, and since one letter represents only one sound, any child who has mastered *hiragana* is capable of reading Japanese. (Ito, 2004)

Thus, many young children learn Japanese as they read manga. What is important to recognize, Ito adds, is that manga help socialize Japanese people by providing them with information on the norms in Japanese society. As Ito explains:

> As the Japanese read manga and experience various events, social situations, and emotions vicariously, they not only entertain themselves, but also learn social skills and gain pragmatic information and knowledge that are necessary for everyday life.

So manga are an important phenomenon in Japan, ranging from certain 'classic' manga that are similar in nature to graphic novels to other kinds of manga that focus on sports, romance, sex and other aspects of life. The Japanese read manga from their earliest years through their old age, and in recent years, manga cafes have sprung up, similar in nature to internet cafes, where people can get food and read manga.

In their article 'Aspects of the Development Towards a Visual Culture in Respect of Comics: Japan', Lee Loveday and Satomi Chiba (1986: 158) offer some statistics about the production of manga in 1986 (when their article appeared in *Comics and Visual Culture*). I am offering their data in a table to simplify matters:

300	Types of manga produced regularly
272 million	Issues of weekly comic magazines sold
950 million	Comic magazines sold in 1981
13%	Amount of weekly allowance spent by high school children
42%	Of Japanese high school children's book collections are manga
1976	Study shows that blue-collar workers spend a third of their leisure time reading manga

These figures are from 30 years ago, so the penetration by manga of the Japanese reading public is, quite possibly, even higher.

In an article on the internet site of *USA Today*, there were some interesting statistics on the sale of manga in 2007. Sales of manga slipped by 4% to slightly more than $4 billion, the fifth year in a row that sales of manga have dropped. There are several reason for this decline. One is that the number of young Japanese has been declining (from more than a third of the population in 1950 to less than 14% in 2007). So there are fewer teenagers to purchase manga. Another reason is that young people are now 'obsessed' with cell phones and are diverted from manga by their cell phones, video games and other electronic media. Finally, some critics suggest that manga are becoming boring and manga artists are not producing exciting and interesting stories. On the other hand, sales of manga in the United States reached $200 million and they are increasingly popular in other countries as well (http://www.usatoday.com/news/world/2007-10-18-manga_N.htm).

The growth of manga

Loveday and Chiba explain that 'the big take-off in the medium really came after the mid-sixties with an intense, often sordid realism frequently focusing upon lust and violence' (1986: 163). When they wrote their article, there were more than 90 erotic manga such as *Sexy Action*, *Manga Strong* and *Gekiga Butcher*. They explain the appeal of manga as follows:

> The fundamental sociopsychological motive that can be attributed to the comic medium's success is its instant provision of escape from

frustration and monotony into a sensorily exciting, self-affirming dream world. The charm is achieved by turning the reader into a voyeur of almost film-like action and forcing his immersion into the experiences of the characters through emotionalized and highly dynamic situations of tension. (Loveday & Chiba, 1986: 168)

They point out that the Japanese spend a great deal of time commuting and use manga to escape from the boredom of travel. They add that manga, which once had social criticism in them, now essentially help young people escape from society and its concerns. One impact of reading manga is that the Japanese now live in what they call an 'eyesight-culture', one that is dominated by visual phenomena (the term they use is *shikakubunka*).

The fact that manga make up approximately a third of all the books published in Japan suggests that though Japan has a high literacy rate, what the Japanese public reads in great measure is generally not of high literary merit. Manga are comic books which means the Japanese spend much of their reading time looking at drawings of characters of various kinds – and seeing everyone from superheroes in action to seeing sexually explicit and sometimes pornographic love stories. The Japanese have a tradition of pornographic art work that dates far back in Japanese history, so seeing pornographic and sexually explicit drawings is nothing new, but the popularity of this kind of art is new. One of the most fascinating erotic Japanese images shows an octopus having sex with a woman, its various tentacles caressing her breasts and one penetrating her vagina.

In addition, manga are narratives which means that the Japanese public is exposed to extremely large numbers of narratives over the

Manga store in Kyoto

years – especially since Japanese people tend to spend long periods of time commuting and reading these 'telephone-book-sized manga' (as they are frequently described). Narratives may have a primary entertainment value, but they are also ways in which we learn about the world. What is interesting about manga is that they have relatively little dialogue in them but are rich in onomatopoetic sound-effects words, which explains why some students of manga suggest it is more appropriate to think of them as cartoons than comic strips.

The significance of manga in Japan

In their book *The Japanese Today*, Edward Reischauer and Marius B. Jansen speculate about the significance of manga for Japanese culture. They write:

> Once Japanese could be seen reading everywhere, on trains, in waiting rooms, and wherever else the situation allowed. They might have been called the 'readingest' people in the world. But many of these former readers are now engrossed in the pictures and inarticulate grunts of cartoons. Originally limited to children, their popularity spread to college students, and now sedate businessmen and housewives can be seen devouring them. They run from imaginative adventure stories of all types to equally diverse stories of love or pornographic appeal. What this all means is hard to fathom: a broadening of the public attracted to print, a lessening of the attention span and a lowering of taste produced by television, a revulsion against serious reading by people overburdened by the pressures of school and the workplace, or a sign of the vulgarization of mass society. (Reischauer & Jansen, 1994: 222–223)

One could argue all of the above, and what makes matters more interesting is that large numbers of people all over the world now have developed a passion for Japanese manga and for the related art form of animé.

Ito points out something interesting about manga, at the end of his article – which was based upon interviewing 40 Japanese people, from 14 to 53 years of age. He discovered that manga readers felt very strongly about their manga and that people who read the same manga bonded with one another. Manga, he said, became the 'collective consciousness' of many Japanese people. He added, 'many interesting manga stories have the effect of drugs and soap operas on paper: they are highly addictive' (2004: 402). That may help explain why the manga play such an important role in contemporary Japanese popular culture, and culture in general. Manga also play a significant role in what might be called the current 'Japanese-ification' of the world, since their popularity is now of global proportions. They are part of a 'popular culture imperialism' in which Japanese manga, video games and other aspects of Japanese popular culture are now spread throughout the world and are increasingly playing a large role in the popular culture of countries everywhere.

When I was in Japan I made a half a dozen short videos about Japanese culture that I uploaded to YouTube. Since my return to the United States, I have received a number of messages from people who look around the site for videos about Japanese culture and send me complimentary messages about my video on Manga, writing things like 'paradise' or 'where is that place? I'm dying to go there'. I have not received a message about any of my other videos, which suggests that manga play an important role in the consciousness and lifestyles of young people in the United States and other countries as well.

Otaku

There is another matter related to manga and Japanese character that is of interest. And that is the obsessive–compulsive personality of many collectors of manga, the related art form, animé and other kinds of popular culture as well. In Peter Carey's book *Wrong about Japan*, he writes about the significance of the term 'Otaku'. As he explains:

> Otaku: an animé fan. The term literally means 'you' in a very formal sense. In Japan it has come to mean people who are obsessed with something to the point where they have few personal relationships. The nature of the obsessions can be anything from animé to computers. In Japan otaku has the same negative connotations as nerd. In America, however, it refers specifically to hardcore anime fans without any negative connotations. (Carey, 2006: 60)

This obsessive personality structure is something we will see in other areas of Japanese culture and society and reaches its tragic end in the behaviour of the hikikomori, the young Japanese hermits who seclude themselves in their parents' flats and houses and withdraw from Japanese society for months and sometimes for years. The Otaku are signifiers, we might say, of the many transformations that have taken place in Japanese society and culture.

Shinjinrui

Shinjinrui, or 'the new race', are young people in Japan, generally below 30 years, who wear wild clothes and have brightly coloured hair, a look similar to what was known in Britain and America, when it was popular, as 'punk'. Tourists who visit the Shibuya section of Tokyo will often see these youth congregating in the area, shopping, texting on their cell phones and looking for excitement. The Shinjinrui are Japanese rebels who have no regards for the cultural norms that shape the behaviour of other young people. Calling them the 'new race' is interesting due to the powerful feelings found in Japan that the people must maintain racial purity. Calling the Shinjinrui a new 'race' suggests that they are something foreign in Japanese society. The Shinjinrui are individualists in a group-centred, conformist culture and reject the lifestyle of more conventional Japanese youth. Thus, the Shinjinrui, when they do work, have part-time jobs and are not interested in becoming salarymen and having full-time jobs in big corporations.

Some critics of Japanese culture suggest that these youth should be pitied, because they grew up, like many children and young people in Japan, in 'fatherless' homes – homes where the father worked so long at his job that he spent relatively little time with his children. This 'fatherlessness' leads to overly strong bonds with their mothers for children of both sexes. Many parents, feeling guilty about their neglect of their children, try to make up for their neglect by giving their children money, which has led to excessive materialism in many Japanese youth, who are self-indulgent and spend freely to buy whatever it is they desire.

We find, then, an ironic situation in many Japanese families in which fathers work endlessly to provide for their families and their children do not want to work at all and spend endlessly to satisfy their whims and wants. Consumer cultures are identified with postmodern societies and the free spending Japanese youth can be seen as products of postmodernism's impact on Japanese culture and society. The growth of subcultures such as the Shinjinrui and the 'Shibuya girls' who hang around Shibuya is a reflection of the breakdown of the overarching belief systems that characterize modernist societies and that once functioned effectively to shape Japanese youth. Some scholars of Japanese culture argue that it is not as conformist and anti-individualist as we think, but this seems to be a minority view.

Postmodernism in Japan

A French postmodernism scholar, Jean-François Lyotard, characterized postmodernism as involving 'incredulity toward metanarratives', by which he meant a lack of belief in overarching philosophical systems and narratives that used to shape peoples' lives. In postmodernist societies such as the United States and Japan, people create their own narratives and reject metanarratives. This leads, among other things, to the development of various subcultures like the Shinjinrui and Otaku in Japan, who can be viewed as signifiers of postmodern societies.

In postmodernist societies, people spend a great deal of time fashioning and refashioning their identities and that involves continual expenditures for new clothes, hairstyles and electronic gear, among other things. Lyotard writes that eclecticism is a dominant feature of postmodern society. He writes, in his book *The Postmodern Condition: A Report on Knowledge*, about the importance of this phenomenon:

> Eclecticism is the degree zero of contemporary general culture: one listens to reggae, watches a western, eat McDonald's food for lunch and local cuisine for dinner, wears Paris perfume in Tokyo and 'retro' clothes in Hong Kong; knowledge is a matter of TV games. It is easy to find a public for eclectic works. By becoming kitsch, art panders to the confusion which reigns in the 'taste' of the patrons. Artists, gallery owners, critics, and public wallow together in the 'anything goes', and the epoch is one of slackening. This realism of the 'anything goes' is in fact that of money; in the absence of aesthetic criteria, it remains possible and useful to assess the value of works of art according to the profits they yield … As for taste, there is no need to be delicate when one speculates or entertains oneself. (Lyotard, 1984: 76)

He adds that writers and artists in postmodern societies work without rules, which also, I would suggest, applies to the everyday lives of people. When there are no grand narratives and no rules, people create their own narrative and shape their lives according to their whims. Thus postmodernism helps explain the existence of subcultures like the Shinjinrui and other so-called deviant groups in contemporary Japan. These groups reflect what postmodern theorists call a 'crisis of legitimation' in the societies in which they are found.

One other aspect of postmodernist societies that Lyotard calls attention to is that they are consumer societies. In the chaos and confusion of postmodern societies, the only thing we can be certain of is what things cost. A prominent theoretician of postmodernism, Fredric Jameson argues that what we call postmodernism is really another name for an advanced form of capitalism.

Some scholars see the Shinjinrui and other subcultures in Japan as the vanguard of a social and cultural revolution taking place in Japan while others see them as anomic and alienated individuals who have not, for one reason or another, been socialized correctly. The existence of subcultures like the Shinjinrui and the Otaku, along with other aspects of Japanese culture such as its high suicide rate and its 'parasite children', suggests that there are enormous unresolved social and cultural problems in Japan. The trains may run on time and Japanese culture seems orderly and safe to tourists, but if you scratch beneath the surface, in many respects, Japanese society has serious problems that continue to plague it.

High-Tech Toilets

We have to realize that objects have a great deal to tell us about ourselves and about the cultures in which they are found. Objects, or technically speaking 'material culture', are a form of culture and thus can be analysed and interpreted the same way we interpret others aspects of culture, such as myths, rituals, food preferences, ceremonies and religious practices. As Ernest Dichter, generally considered the 'father of motivation research', comments in his book *The Strategy of Desire*:

> The objects which surround us do not simply have utilitarian aspects; rather they serve as a kind of mirror which reflects our own image. Objects which surround us permit us to discover more and more aspects of ourselves ... In a sense, therefore, the knowledge of the soul of things is possibly a direct and new and revolutionary way of discovering the soul of man. (Dichter, 2002: 91)

Many other scholars have commented about the significance of objects.

Richard S. Latham, an industrial designer, offers other insights into objects and artefacts. In his article 'The Artifact as a Cultural Cipher', he explains:

> Artifacts and useful objects are a part of all recorded history. They are devised, invented, and made as adjuncts to the human being's ability to accomplish work or enjoy pleasure. A close examination of any object is a graphic description of the level of intelligence, manual dexterity, and artistic comprehension of the civilization that produced it. It can reflect, as well, the climate, religious beliefs, form of government, the natural materials at hand, the structure of commerce, and the extent of man's scientific and emotional sophistication. (Latham, 1966: 258)

All of these observations are read out of a simple artefact by the skilled archaeologist with or without benefit of the written word. All of these things are read out of objects every day by the unskilled layman. It is the silent language of the senses.

Technically and semiotically speaking, objects (and I consider objects and artefacts to be the same thing) are signs: the objects are signifiers and what we find when we analyse these objects is their signifieds.

The Toto Washlet toilet

Thus, the Toto Washlet 'high-tech' toilet, which sells for between $2000 and $4000, is an artefact of considerable interest. The company makes a number of different toilets, but the most important of these toilets, for our concerns, are their 'high-tech' Washlet toilets that have features such as noisemakers that create a flushing sound to mask whatever sounds you may be making as you sit on the toilet; a device that squirts warm water onto your anus, so you do not need to use toilet paper; a blow-dryer that warms your rear end after you have been squirted with warm water as you sit on the toilet; a self-cleaning device for toilets; coatings that resist germs; buttons that open and close the lids on toilets automatically (a button for men that lifts the lid and the seat; a button for women that only lifts the lid); warmers for seats so you do not sit on a cold toilet seat.

Toto also sells a portable $100 'Travel Washlet' that squirts water (that one can warm at home) to approximate a regular Washlet toilet when travelling. Ironically, approximately a third of Japanese people live in homes that do not have flush toilets, so we have polar extremes here: some Japanese homes without flush toilets and those with ultra-modern 'high-tech' toilets.

Japanese high-tech toilet

Japanese perfectionism

Clotaire Rapaille believes that because of the pressures of population, the Japanese have developed a perfectionist mentality. Thus, for Rapaille, there is a pressure in Japanese society to perfect everything – including, we might add, toilets. He adds that Japanese feel that being in good health is a social obligation, since that will enable Japanese to contribute to the well-being of their families and communities. As he writes:

> The Japanese are obsessive about remaining healthy, and they feel a powerful sense of guilt if they fall ill ... Japanese children will always apologize to their parents for getting sick, for they know illness may cause them to fall behind. In this culture, you don't just wash your hands to stay clean, but also out of a sense of duty to yourself as a servant of the culture and to prevent someone else from getting sick because of you. (Rapaille, 2006: 81–82)

So there are cultural imperatives or 'codes' behind Japanese behaviour in bathrooms, and these codes are connected to the Japanese psyche.

For a psychoanalytical perspective, these toilets reflect something quite different – namely a loathing of faeces and other kinds of bodily excretions. Blowing one's nose in public in Japan is considered undignified and people who wish to blow their noses are told to find a private place to do so. Japan is famous for being clean and this cleanliness is tied to a reflection of this cultural anxiety the Japanese have about faeces and bodily excretions and other kinds of 'dirt', in general.

Purity in Japan

There seems to be a great concern for maintaining 'purity' in Japan, and this includes also the way certain groups in Japan, such as the Koreans who have lived in Japan for long periods of time, are shunned by the Japanese. Body fluids and all who are 'non-Japanese' (*gaijin*, the term for foreigners, is composed of '*gai*' outside and '*jin*' persons, that is 'outside persons') are excluded from that which is acceptable in Japan. Indeed, some groups in Japan are described as *ningai* or people who are 'outside of humanity'. It is often the case that there is a connection between hierarchical societies and a stress on purity (and fear of contamination) in various areas of life. We see this in India where, in earlier times, Brahmins avoided even the shadow of untouchables and untouchables were not supposed to look at them.

And yet, it is not unusual for Japanese men to urinate on the street at night after their drinking bouts or to vomit, leaving 'Japanese pizzas' on streets and in subway cars. So you have a most unusual combination of extreme fastidiousness about body fluids, especially urine and faeces, in Japanese culture, yet violations of these codes are accepted by drunken Japanese men, just as being drunk, after a night of drinking with one's coworkers, is also tolerated as is playing *Pachinko*, which is a form of gambling but one that is overlooked and redefined by political authorities in Japan. There is a widespread willingness to overlook certain aspects of life that softens the often harsh, over-regulated, prohibition-filled, nature of Japanese culture and society.

Vending Machines

Vending machines (*jidoohanbaiki*) are found all over Japan, and visitors to the country encounter them as they visit various Japanese cities and towns. It is estimated that there is one vending machine for every 23 persons in Japan – the highest number of vending machines per capita of any country and more than 6 million of these machines in the country. In part, this is because Japanese houses are generally so small that they do not have a lot of room in which to store things but also because vending machines make an incredible number of products easily and immediately available to the Japanese public. The Japanese now are used to having these machines around and they play an important role in Japanese consumer culture, much like the ubiquitous 7-Eleven stores and other convenience stores. These machines are often found outside of 7-Eleven stores, as a matter of fact.

These vending machines are a reflection of the high cost of floor space in stores in Japan and of the low crime rate in Japan, which means that few vending machines are vandalized. Since some of the products sold by vending machines involve sexual matters, the machines also provide anonymity for the purchaser. This anonymity applies to products such as pornographic videos, condoms and used schoolgirl panties, known as *burusera* in Japan (*bura* means bloomers and *sera* means sailors, which applies to the design of these panties). This fetishism focused on used schoolgirl panties is a reflection of what has been called the 'Lolita' complex in many Japanese men, who find young, childish, school girlish and 'cute' women desirable.

The range of products sold in these vending machines is remarkable. One site on the internet, photomann (www.photomann.com/Japan/

Photo of vending machines

machines) carries photographs of typical vending machines and shows that they contain such products as:

Eggs	Kerosene	Dry ice
Umbrellas	Soft drinks	Beer, alcohol
Name cards	Cigarettes	Batteries
Hot ramen	Toilet paper	Vegetables
Energy drinks	Flowers	Newspapers
Condoms	Fried foods	Subway tickets
Hot popcorn	Porno videos	Horse race betting
Used schoolgirls panties	Rice	Ice cream

The photomann site has photographs of 50 different vending machines, although there is some overlap in the products found in these machines.

Vending machines and the mechanization of Japanese society

The widespread use of these vending machines reflects the mechanization of Japanese society that has grown quickly, since the machines started becoming popular in the 1960s. One reason for this is that the population of Japan is shrinking, so there are fewer workers available to sell products to Japanese consumers. These machines also reflect the fact that the

Japanese are stressed in many different areas of life and are thus drawn to the machines which enable Japanese consumers to purchase products instantaneously and not have to bother with looking in stores and dealing with clerks. This impersonal aspect of vending machines is useful in cases where you do not want anyone else to know what you have bought. One can purchase condoms, pornographic videos and used schoolgirl panties without anyone else knowing.

Psychoanalytically speaking, we may wonder whether there is in Japan a need for immediate gratification of their desires and wishes in some areas to counter the stress that many Japanese feel in their work and homes. These machines are only part of the mechanization found in Japan, where various devices such as electronic rice cookers and an endless number of electronic gizmos, including bread-makers, rice cookers and cell phones, are part of everyday life. What these vending machines do, also, is turn Japan into a gigantic open-air department store. Instead of a large department store with various products inside it, the products have been transferred into vending machines that are now found on the pavements in Japanese cities and towns. There are still many department stores in Japan, which sell many products that cannot be sold in vending machines and provide many other products and services which Japanese consumers value. But these machines are a $50 billion industry and thus play an important role in the Japanese economy.

7-Eleven Convenience Stores

Visitors to Japan cannot help but notice the enormous number of 7-Eleven stores and other convenience stores such as am/pm and Family Mart as well. They are ubiquitous. It is interesting to know that the first Japanese 7-Eleven opened in 1974. The stores originated in Dallas, Texas, in 1927 and were purchased by a Japanese company, Ito-Yokado, in the 1980s, according to information on the Wikipedia site that deals with 7-Eleven stores in Japan. In 2005, the 7-Eleven stores (all over the world) took in $43 billion in revenues.

The statistics about 7-Eleven stores are quite astonishing. There are now something like 30,000 7-Eleven stores in 19 countries. As of 2008, there are approximately 12,000 7-Eleven stores in Japan, with more than 1500 7-Eleven stores found in Tokyo. There are 7100 7-Eleven stores in North America and the Japanese stores, while half the size of the American stores, sell twice as much as they do. Their inventory is around a third of that found in American stories, and their product line is also quite different. The Japanese stores sell a great deal of food, but also iPods and they will take orders for Rolex watches. It turns out that the 7-Eleven stores are the top food products retailer in Japan.

A *New York Times* article by James Sterngold, 'New Japanese Lesson: Running a 7-11', written in 1991, points out that the Japanese stores are successful because they are run in a highly disciplined manner, with 'just-in-time' shipments of goods and a well-developed computer system that keeps track of inventory and consumer preferences with a point-of-sale system, that records which lunch boxes are selling well and the age and sex of those who purchase these lunch boxes. This enables the proprietors of the stores and the 7-Eleven management to determine consumer demand with a high degree of accuracy. The stores produce a great deal of cash and what the 7-Eleven management does with that cash is the key to the chain's success. One commentator suggested that the 7-Eleven stores are like banks, and the corporation's basic problem involves maximizing the cash the stores pull in from their customers.

In a sense, without stretching credulity too much, we can think of these 7-Eleven stores in Japan as being gigantic multi-product vending machines, or collections of vending machines under one roof, maintained by human beings, who sell products to consumers and keep detailed records about what they have sold and the demographics of their customers for everything they purchase. When the Japanese develop robots to collect money and record the demographics of the purchasers of each product, the evolution of the stores will be complete.

Pachinko

There are an estimated 18,000 *Pachinko* parlours scattered throughout Japan. It is commonly held that these parlours are owned by Japanese of Korean descent (who are treated like pariahs by the Japanese) and have connections with yakuza – criminal elements in Japan. Technically speaking, playing *Pachinko* is not gambling since players do not receive money for winning. Instead, they win little things that have hardly any intrinsic value, but these objects can be exchanged for money in places that all *Pachinko* players know.

Psychological immersion and addiction

Pachinko games are similar to pin ball machines, except that unlike pinball machines, which are horizontal, they are vertical and players play in large rooms full of these machines, which are extremely noisy and loud. The aura in these parlours is similar to that found in gambling casinos in

Pachinko parlour

the United States, where hundreds of people play slot machines, also in a brightly lit electro-neon ambience, although *Pachinko* parlours are much noisier than slot machine emporia. It is possible to suggest that the flashing lights and noise in these parlours play a role in inducing certain kinds of semi-hypnotic trance-like behaviours, which helps explain why players keep pouring money into these machines. There is a kind of immersion, similar to that experienced by video game players, which takes place. And the *Pachinko* games provide increasing gratifications as players win leading to a form of addiction, found also in video games.

Robert W. Kubey, a communications scholar, writes about video games in his article 'Television Dependence, Diagnosis, and Prevention: With Commentary on Video Games, Pornography, and Media Education':

> As with television, the games offer the player a kind of escape, and as with television, players learn quickly that they momentarily feel better when playing computer games, hence a kind of psychological reinforcement develops. (Kubey, 1996: 242)

But video and computer games also have particular characteristics that make children and adults especially likely to report that they are 'addicted' to them. There is the general challenge posed by the game and the wish to overcome it and succeed, and there is the critical characteristic that the games are designed to minutely increase in challenge and difficulty along with the increasing ability of the player.

What Kubey points out is that games often have, within them, means which enhance the feeling of well-being in players that ultimately can lead to addiction.

Inside a *Pachinko* parlour

This passion for *Pachinko* eats up around 20% of the typical household income in some rural areas and is the largest industry in Japan – larger than the automobile industry and the computer industry, according to figures found in Alex Kerr's *Lost Japan*. He sees *Pachinko* games as a kind of meditation and the arrangement of pins in the machines as similar in nature to mandalas – thus suggesting a mystical aspect to playing the games, and suggests that the *Pachinko* aesthetic has now influenced many other areas of Japanese life such as architecture and graphic design. It is estimated that a number of divorces in Japan are caused, one way or another, by *Pachinko* addicts. As he writes:

> The overwhelming hold of *Pachinko* can hardly exaggerated. In some rural districts, it accounts for up to twenty per cent of disposable household income. *Pachinko* is now the single largest industry, outpacing cars and computers, and Japan's richest man by some calculations is a man whose company produces most of the machines. *Pachinko* has developed its own style, consisting of brightly colored rooms laced with constructions of chrome and neon, and oversize plastic statues of animals or gods of good luck. It has become the preferred style of

Japanese entertainment: you find it everywhere from restaurants and bars to the sets of most popular TV programs. It influences architecture, and is the inspiration behind many a glitzy hotel lobby. Kyoto Tower is very much in this *Pachinko* mode. (Kerr, 1996: 209–210)

The status of these games reflects a certain aspect of Japanese culture that refuses to recognize reality or, more precisely, that prefers to mask reality and avoid telling the truth about certain things.

The great Kurosawa film, *Ikiru*, deals with a man waiting in a medical clinic, who has cancer, but his doctor refuses to tell him so. This is because many Japanese doctors do not believe that they should tell their patients when they have cancer or other serious illnesses. The grief with which college-aged Japanese boys and girls react to notices of their grades, after they have taken the 'exam-hell' tests that will determine which university they will attend, shows that in some areas Japanese culture cannot shield everyone from bitter truths, or does not care to do so.

Pachinko is, everyone in Japan recognizes, a form of gambling. Gambling is illegal in Japan, but it is allowed, thanks to the ruse of the payment for winning being trivial little gifts – which everyone knows can be turned in for money. We might see this *Pachinko* phenomenon as the revenge of the Korean Japanese, who own many of these *Pachinko* parlours, for being ostracized and discriminated against by the Japanese public. The Japanese government may allow these parlours to exist because they see them as ways of distracting many Japanese people from the pressures they feel and from their discontents.

Pachinko and the Japanese temperament

But the government, it would seem, does not consider the tragic consequences that the Japanese passion for *Pachinko* is having on large numbers of Japanese families and Japanese culture and society. Kerr offers a hypothesis to explain the phenomenon. He suggests that the Japanese national school system creates a homogeneous society in which everyone more or less thinks the same and looks the same. In such a society full of people leading, as he puts it, 'mediocre' lives, low-level entertainments such as *Pachinko* are well suited for the Japanese temperament. As he writes:

Why has pachinko swept Japan? It can hardly be the excitement of gambling, since the risks and rewards are so small. During the hours spent in front of a pachinko machine, there is an almost total lack of stimulation other than the occasional rush of ball bearings. There is no thought, no movement; you have no control over the flow of balls, apart from

> holding a little lever which shoots them to the top of the machine; you sit there, enveloped in a cloud of heavy cigarette smoke, semi-dazed by the rack of millions of ball bearings falling through machines around you. Pachinko verges on sensory deprivation; It is the ultimate mental numbing, the final victory of the educational system. (Kerr, 1996: 223)

The Zen rock garden and the *Pachinko* parlour may be seen as two polar opposites in Japanese culture, and it is the *Pachinko* parlour that is now dominant.

Gift Giving in Japan

Japan is a culture in which giving and receiving gifts is of major importance. That helps explain why Japanese tourists spend so much time and so much money purchasing things to bring back to Japan and give to their friends as gifts. Gifts are a way that Japanese people show their affection for others and help maintain and strengthen relationships between people.

Japanese people like to have their gifts wrapped nicely and one might suggest that it is the idea of the gift and the aesthetics of the gift box that are more important than the actual gift itself. Tourism guides often admonish readers to make sure that the gifts they bring to Japan are nicely wrapped. The guides suggest American tourists bring chocolates, maple syrup or little things that are distinctively American. In Japan, gifts that are in boxes from expensive department stores are especially appreciated. The box from the store and the status of the store signify the esteem in which the gift-giver holds the intended receiver.

In their book *Consumer Behavior: A European Perspective*, Michael Solomon, Gary Bamossy and Soren Askegard offer some insights into Japanese gift giving:

> The importance of gift-giving rituals is underscored by considering Japanese customs, where the wrapping of a gift is as important (if not more so) than the gift itself. The economic value of the gift is secondary to its symbolic meaning. To the Japanese, gifts are viewed as an important aspect of one's duty to others in one's social group. Giving is a moral imperative (known as *giri*). (Solomon *et al.*, 2002: 452–453)

Highly ritualized gift giving occurs during the giving of both household/personal gifts and company/professional gifts. Each Japanese has a well-defined set of relatives and friends with whom he or she shares reciprocal gift-giving obligations (*kosai*).

Giving gifts has a number of functions, such as strengthening relationships and affirming the nature of a relationship.

The social dimensions of gift giving

Gift giving is, in fact, a rather complicated social and cultural phenomenon. In his book, *The Gift: Imagination and the Erotic Life of Property*, Lewis Hyde discusses the work of the French sociologist, Marcel Mauss, who wrote an essay on gifts. Hyde writes:

> Mauss noticed, for one thing, that gift economies tend to be marked by three related obligations: the obligation to give, the obligation to accept, and the obligation to reciprocate. He also pointed out that we should understand gift exchange to be a 'total social phenomenon' – one whose transactions are at one economic, juridical, moral, aesthetic, religious, and mythological, and whose meaning cannot, therefore, be adequately described from the point of view of any single discipline. (Hyde, 1979: xv)

So gift giving is connected to many aspects of Japanese cultural life and is a useful means towards understanding the Japanese psyche and Japanese society.

Gift giving in the United States

In the United States, people give others gifts for birthdays and other life cycle events and especially during the Christmas holidays. The obligation people feel to give others gifts during this period had led to the weeks and months before Christmas being the most important period for sellers of products and services. During this period large numbers of Americans experience a great deal of stress, because gift giving involves calculating what kind of gift to give and how much money to spend for a gift. In her article, 'The Christmas Gift Horse', Sheila Johnson discusses the dilemmas gift givers and those who receive gifts face. If a gift is too cheap, people who receive the gift will feel slighted and if it is too expensive they will feel humiliated or embarrassed, especially if their gift was not as expensive as the gift they received. That is one reason why so many people choose to give liquor or food as gifts. These gifts put those who receive them under less social obligation and they are consumed, so the person receiving these gifts does not need to display them.

Johnson deals with some of the calculations involved by givers and recipients of gifts and writes:

> Aside from the basic decision to give a gift, which in itself may involve some delicate calculations, there are several other questions that must be settled. How much should it cost? Too expensive and the recipient

might be embarrassed or feel obligated to go out and buy you something equally costly; too cheap, and he might feel insulted. What sort of object should it be? A gift reflects the giver's taste, but it can also reflect the impression the giver has formed or the recipient's taste, proving more room for intended and unintended results. (Johnson, 1974: 82)

Gift receivers do the same kinds of calculations, she adds, and points out that they also have to decide whether gift requires them to replay it immediately or in the future and whether it is being given for services rendered or to be rendered in the future.

Rules for giving gifts in Japan

One of the cardinal aspects of gift giving involves reciprocity and in Japan, gifts reflect the web of social connections among individuals, who are constantly giving one another gifts and, in so doing, affirming and intensifying their connections with their friends and their solidarity with their culture. Because of the pressures of population in Japan, the people live in proximity with one another and need to find ways to maintain good relationships. Gift giving is functional, then, in helping Japanese people live and work with one another in a peaceful and orderly way, with a minimum of social disruptions. Gifts in Japan tie people to one another and enmesh everyone there in a net of social obligations. But the need to continually be giving gifts place a certain amount of stress, especially when Japanese people travel to foreign lands and feel the need to bring back gifts (*omiyage*) for their family members and friends. That is why Japanese tourists devote so much time and money to buying gifts.

There are a number of rules one must follow when giving or receiving gifts in Japan, although the following codes of behaviour do not necessarily all apply to foreigners, who can be forgiven for making mistakes:

- Give gifts at the end of the visit, not at the start.
- Give gifts with both hands (and accept gifts with both hands).
- Modestly refuse gifts once or twice before accepting them.
- Wrap gifts in pastel colours (avoiding white and red paper and bows)
- Tell those receiving gifts what they are.
- The Japanese believe gifts in pairs are lucky.
- If you give flowers, give an uneven number.
- The person receiving the gift will refuse, at first, but then accept it.
- Minimize the importance of your gift, saying it is 'a little nothing'.
- If invited to a home, bring flowers, cakes or sweets.
- When receiving a gift, do not open it until your guests have left.

Not opening gifts until your guests have departed avoids 'loss of face' if the gift is not one that you think is appropriate for you or one you do not like. If you do not open it and do not want it, you can then recycle it and give the gift to someone else. And that gift you have just received may have been a gift from someone else to the person who gave you the gift. So unopened gifts may circulate for years through your circle of friends and it is possible that the gift you just received was one you gave to someone a number of years ago.

Gift giving in any culture involves all kinds of calculations about the style and taste level of the people who will be receiving a gift and the amount of money that is proper to spend on the gift or gifts. The Japanese have many times in the year when gift giving is appropriate and always expect to get gifts from their friends and relatives who have returned from trips, just as they expect to get gifts for friends and relatives when they take trips. Gifts in Japan are a highly formalized and ritualized form of behaviour that cement ties between friends and family members and it may be that the act of giving the gift is actually more important than the particular gifts that are received.

Gift giving and the Melanesian Kula

When I think about gift giving in Japan I cannot help but compare it to a similar phenomenon analysed by anthropologist Bronislaw Malinowski in his classic study *Argonauts of the Western Pacific*, published first in 1921. His book dealt with the Kula, a form of exchange in which long, red-shelled necklaces called *soulava* circulated in one direction through a number of widely scattered islands in the western Pacific and white shell bracelets called *mwali* circulated in the other direction. Malinowski wrote that two of the cardinal rules of the Kula are that gifts must be repaid by counter-gifts of equal value after a certain amount of time (the amount of time between a gift and counter-gift can vary), and that decisions about the value of counter-gifts are left up to the person giving them.

Malinowski's description of the Kula suggests why I see Japanese gift giving and the Kula as similar in nature. He writes:

> Each of these articles, as it travels in its own directions on the closed circuit, meets on its way articles of the other class, and is constantly being exchanged for them. Every movement of the Kula articles, every detail of the transactions is fixed and regulated by a set of traditional rules and conventions, and some acts of the Kula are accompanied by an elaborate magic ritual and public ceremonies.... (Malinowski, 1921/1961: 81)

Malinowski then explains that the Kula had an important impact, in that it bound those who participated in it – even though they were unaware of the scope of the institution – into long-term relationships.

He writes:

> Sociologically, though transacted between tribes differing in language, culture and probably even in race, it is based on a fixed and permanent status, on a partnership which binds into couples some thousands of individuals. This partnership is a lifelong relationship, it implies various mutual duties and privileges, and constitutes a type of inter-tribal relationship on an enormous scale. (Malinowski, 1921/1961: 85)

This description suggests that although the Kula and gift giving in Japan are similar in many ways, they both have the same function – establishing and supporting relationships among individuals by binding them into a number of mutual duties and obligations.

The Kula, Malinowski explains, exchanges articles which have no practical utility, so it is also similar to gift giving in Japan, where the objects given (and in some cases passed on to others) are not based on needs but function to facilitate and consolidate friendships and relationships. In some cases in Japan, the distinction between a gift and a bribe is hard to see, so some gift giving actually functions as bribes to bosses, public officials and other people whose goodwill can be of assistance, one way or another.

Gift giving also has a significant economic impact in Japan, where families might spend between 1% and 3% of their total family income on gifts. It is estimated that the two gift-giving periods, *ochugen* in the summer and *oseibo* in the winter, contribute around 60% of the profits of department stores in Tokyo and the figure is probably similar for other cities. Gift certificates from prestigious department stores are a popular gift, which relieves the person giving the gift of having to determine what kind of gift to give.

In this respect, the summer and winter gift-giving periods are similar to the Christmas gift-giving period in the United States, which is when stores make a considerable percentage of their profits. Gifts in the United States are also given at various stages in the life cycle, as in Japan. The obligation to give gifts is also responsible for some Japanese avoiding travel to their hometowns and hiding their travel plans from friends, so as to escape the burden of having to buy gifts for large number of people. So gift giving in Japan is an institution of major consequence in the lives of typical Japanese citizens and plays an important role in the economy as well.

100 Yen Stores

These stores, which sell everything for 100 yen, became very popular when the Japanese economic 'bubble' burst in the 1990s. There is also a 5 yen tax, so you end up paying 105 yen for things you purchase in these stores. The Daiso chain, which has 60% of the market for this kind of store, has around 2500 stores in Japan and is opening 20–30 new stores each month. Daiso describes itself as 'Japan's Number One Ranking Livingware Supplier' (http://www.daiso-sangyo.co.jp/english/products) on its website. Daiso carries 90,000 different products and adds 1000 news ones each month. Its sales in 2005 were more than 320 billion yen. If each patron of a 100 yen store in Japan purchased 320 yen's worth of goods or approximately three items on a visit to a store, then that would add up to a billion transactions a year. The 100 yen stores range in size from tiny hole-in-the-wall outlets to some that are very large, occupying more than one storey in a building.

These stores can sell their products for 100 yen because they buy in huge quantities from China, India, Brazil and other countries, and are

100 yen shop in Kyoto

willing to make smaller profits than other stores that have similar products because the 100 yen stores have such a high volume. The 100 yen stores often locate near supermarkets and in spaces that are eventually going to be occupied by more conventional stores.

America also has so-called dollar stores, but they often have merchandize that is more expensive than a dollar, and some Japanese 100 yen store chains are now experimenting with pricier products as well. That is because other kinds of stores are matching their prices, selling some products now at 100 yen. The 100 yen stores are not only popular with Japanese people but also a big attraction for foreign tourists, who are curious to see what is available (and might be a good souvenir or gift for friends and relatives back home) in notoriously expensive – but not always, thanks to 100 yen stores – Japan.

Department Stores (Hyakkaten or Departōs)

Department stores (hyakkaten or '100 goods' stores) occupy the other end of the consumer culture spectrum in Japan, being large 'full-service' emporia with a variety of different kinds of goods and services being available under one roof. They usually have a food hall and a grocery in the basement, where it is possible to sample some of the foods on sale. These food halls are crammed with delicious cakes, confections, delicatessen items and are a food lover's paradise. They bring in around a quarter of the revenues for the stores in which they are found, so they are very important.

There is an air of festivity and excitement in these food halls, since there are cooks, bakers and others making things and setting out displays. The ambience of plenty is infectious; part of the charm comes from this activity and the sense of nostalgia many Japanese feel for the way stores were in earlier times. The food halls sell many products at deep discounts just before closing time, so tourists who want to stock up on goodies and, perhaps, get something for dinner if they are tired of eating in restaurants, can save a good deal of money by going to these food halls just before five o'clock.

The 'departōs' (as they are also known in Japan) also sell clothing, cosmetics, shoes, electronic gear, kitchen appliances and expensive watches and jewellery. They have travel agencies and provide other services as well, such as having restaurants with different kinds of foods on their top floors.

There are usually legions of women, wearing uniforms and white gloves, who work in these stores, smiling and bowing, since in Japanese

Inside a 100 yen store

department stores, the customer truly is king, or since this is Japan, emperor. A visit to a Japanese department tour enables a tourist to see what things cost in Japan and gain some insights into Japanese culture and society. The first time I went to Japan, a number of years ago, I was amazed at how expensive household appliances such as stoves, refrigerators and washing machines were – and how small they were. But small appliances are needed since the size of the average house or flat in Japan, especially in cities, is so small.

The department stores in Japan have been experiencing sales declines for the past decade, in part because of competition from many smaller stores, which do not have the high overhead the department stores have and can sell goods for less than department stores can. This is happening in many countries. It costs a considerable amount of money to provide the level of services that the Japanese department stores have. But gifts from 'prestige' department stores are highly valued in Japan, where people are very status conscious, and department stores make a high percentage of their profits during the two main gift-giving periods.

These stores are tourist attractions in their own right, since they offer tourists the chance to see what Japanese consumers pay for the various goods and products they purchase. By American standards, the things in Japanese stores are quite expensive, because the dollar is so weak against the yen. We are always amazed at the cost of melons and other fruit in Japan.

Expensive melons in Japan are used as gifts

It may be that Japanese department stores help perpetuate the belief American tourists have that it is a very expensive country to visit. That is because, as we saw in my earlier chapter on tourism in Japan, shopping is one of the main activities of tourists wherever they go.

So, while it is possible now to travel in Japan at a moderate cost, it is probably the experiences of many tourists in department stores that reinforce the belief that Japan is extremely expensive. As the euro gets stronger, it turns out that travel in Japan has now become relatively reasonable, for while there are hotels in Tokyo and other Japanese cities that charge $500 a room, there are many that are available for around $100–$150 and for around $80 in business hotels. With the money foreign tourists save in their (relatively speaking) moderately priced hotel rooms in Japan, they have more money to spend in department stores.

Comparison of department stores and temples

It is possible to see department stores as secularized versions of temples, since they have a number of similarities, though their goals are not the same. I spell out some of these similarities and differences in the chart that follows.

Department store	*Temple*
Secular	Sacred
Pop 'selling' music	Sacred 'sounds' and music
Sells goods and services	'Sells' religion
Clerks	Priests
Uniforms	Costumes
Shoppers seek sales	Visitors seek salvation
Passion to consume	Passion to have good luck, be saved
Pay for goods	Give donations
Perfume	Incense
Consumer lust	Religious passion

This chart helps explain why shopping in Japanese department stores is the kind of experience it is, for visiting these gigantic stores has much in common with visiting shrines and temples, although the purpose of visits to department stores is quite different from going to temples and shrines.

The basement food halls, full of delicious foods and confections, have a Garden of Edenesque paradisical quality to them. In medieval Europe, according to Stanley Marcus, one of the founders of Neiman Marcus, the cathedrals were also centres of commerce, so the connection between department stores and religious buildings has a long history. I was on a radio call-in show with him some years ago and when I asked him about my theory relating cathedrals and department stores, he explained that it was quite reasonable because of the historic connection between the two.

The Tokyo Subway Map

Tokyo, often described as an ugly, concrete jungle, is the largest city in the world, with a population of around 35 million people in the greater Tokyo area, and Tokyo's subway or route map is probably the most complicated one in the world. One reason why the system is complicated is because the Tokyo Metro has nine different lines: Ginza, Marunouchi,

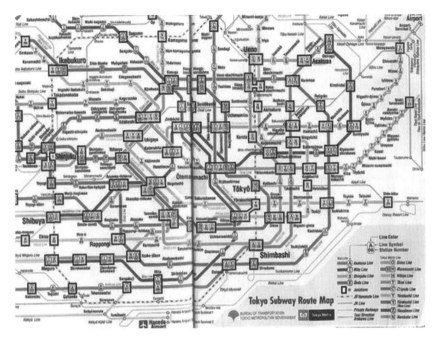

Detail of subway map of Tokyo

Hibiya, Tozai, Chiyoda, Yurakucho, Hanzomon, Namboku and Yurakucho (new line).

In addition, there are five other lines not part of the Tokyo Metro that connect with it: Toei Oedo, Toei Asakusa, Toei Mita, Toei Shinjuku and the Yurikamome Line. There is also the Yamanote or Yamate [either way is fine] line that circles through all of Tokyo. Since these lines all cross one another at various points, and since each line has a separate colour to show its route, you find that the route map has 12 different colours. Some of these colours are difficult to separate from one another. Adding to the complexity is the fact that many stations have letters and numbers underneath them in little boxes and some of these boxes are attached to other boxes. Sometimes you find three, four or five boxes with letters and numbers attached to one another.

The size of Tokyo

The greater Tokyo area is 15,000 ha^2, which is a third larger than greater Los Angeles, which is approximately 10,000 ha^2. (One hectare is approximately 2.47 acres.) Tokyo's area is approximately 55 miles by 15 miles or about 800 square miles in size. Its outline looks like a gigantic elongated oval, which means that some residents in the outer fringes of the city have two and three hour commutes every day. The central city area of Tokyo is only 620 ha^2 compared with 1220 ha^2 for Los Angeles. What these figures mean is that the central city area of Tokyo is relatively small, and this explains why the central city sections of Tokyo are so crowded and why the subway cars in Tokyo are so crammed with people.

Photographs of white gloved guards in subways 'cramming' people into subway cars are one of the more memorable symbols of Tokyo and its subway system and are often found on websites and in guidebooks on Japan. Some Japanese men have used the crowded conditions to grope Japanese women and now there are cars reserved for women and children to alleviate this problem.

Roland Barthes on Tokyo's Empty Centre

The interesting thing about the centre of Tokyo, as Roland Barthes explains in *Empire of Signs*, is that it is empty. He writes:

> The city I am talking about (Tokyo) offers this precious paradox: it does possess a center but this center is empty. The entire city turns around a site both forbidden and indifferent, a residence concealed beneath foliage, protected by moats, inhabited by an emperor who is never seen, which is to say, literally, by no one knows who. Daily, in their rapid, energetic, bullet-like trajectories, the taxies avoid this circle, whose low crest, the visible form of invisibility, hides the sacred 'nothing'. One of the two most powerful cities of modernity is thereby built around an opaque ring of walls, streams, roofs, and trees whose center is no more than an evaporated notion, subsisting here, not in order to radiate power but to give the entire urban movement the support of its central emptiness, forcing traffic to make a perpetual detour. (Barthes, 1970/1982: 30)

This passage is one of the most frequently quoted passages in the book. And while the emperor and the royal family are no longer as hidden as they were in 1970, when Barthes published his book, the empty space in the centre of Tokyo still exists and still has a sacred quality to it. It is interesting to note that the Imperial Palace is in the exact centre of the subway map and has the largest lettering of anything on the map. Barthes also discusses the significance of metro stations, which he believes gives each area of Tokyo where they are found a focal point.

The Tokyo subway is famous because it was the site of a terrible terrorist attack with Sarin gas by the cult Aum Shinrikyo. This event strengthened a popular stereotype about the Japanese people that many people in the Western world have, as exemplified in the La Barre quotation found in an earlier chapter, that there is an element of fanaticism in their character. If the Tokyo subway system represents logic and rationality of the highest order, and the system is a remarkable engineering achievement, the attack on it by the Aum Shinrikyo represents the other side of Japanese character, an irrationality and madness that dumbfounded everyone, since many of the members of the cult were professional men and women who had good educations. Symbolically, the attack on the subway, whose lines are like the system of veins and arteries that carry blood in the human body, was an attempt to poison the people on the subway trains and, by extension, the whole subway system, which would have devastating consequences for the people in Tokyo.

What makes using the Tokyo subway, despite the complexity of the system, a good way to get places, is its speed and the extreme helpfulness of the Japanese people. I recall that in our first visit to Japan, when my wife and I were looking for the train to Kamakura, we asked someone in the gigantic subway station in Shinjuku where we should go to get it and he actually led us to the place, to make sure we found it. The subway system may seem insane, but the kindness of the Japanese subway riders helps humanize it. And what I found is that after a while, we were able to find our way around the subway system fairly easily.

Semanticists argue that the map is not the territory; that is, it is only a representation of the territory. What the Tokyo subway map reflects is the incredible complexity of the territory – that is, Tokyo – and of the capacity of engineers to deal with the enormous difficulties involved in finding ways to help 35 million people move from one place to another in the city. The largest station, Shinjuko, has 2 million people moving through it every day and is enormous.

Whatever else it may be, the Tokyo subway system is one of the engineering marvels of the world. Perhaps the best way to think about the subway map is to consider it a work of art – some kind of a postmodern collage. It also looks something like the schematic design for a computer chip, except that it is not electrons but people, something like 3 billion of them, who go coursing through it various lines every year.

Fugu and Blue-finned Tuna: Fish Madness in Japan

The fact that Tsukiji, the Tokyo Fish market, is one of the most popular tourist attractions in Tokyo tells us something about the importance of fish in Japanese cuisine and Japanese society. The Japanese have a passion for fish and an obsession with fresh fish and certain desirable fishes, such as blue-finned tuna that are used in making sushi. At the Tokyo fish market, these fish are sold at auctions, early in the morning, at what Americans would consider incredible amounts of money. Blue-finned tuna can weigh as much as 1800 pounds and typically sell for more than $100 a pound. If you look around the internet, you can find photos of rows and rows of these fish, generally with their heads cut off, in the market and videos of trips to the market.

Photograph of fish in store

On rawness in Japanese food

In his book, *Empire of Signs*, the French semiotician and cultural critic Roland Barthes (1982: 20, 22) argues that rawness is

> the tutelary divinity of Japanese food: to it everything is dedicated ... Japanese rawness is essentially visual; it denotes a certain colored state of the flesh or vegetable substance (it being understood that color is never exhausted by a catalogue of tints, but refers to a whole tactility of substance; thus *sashimi* exhibits not so much color as resistances: those which vary the flesh of raw fish, causing it to pass from one end of the tray to the other, through the stations of the soggy, the fibrous, the elastic, the compact, the rough, the slippery). (Barthes, 1982: 20)

If you are going to eat raw fish, quite naturally you would want it to be very fresh, and Barthes does a wonderful job of describing the varying textures of *sashimi* and the importance of it, and other food as well, being visually attractive. The Japanese attitude towards fish can be diagnosed as a kind of collective fish madness, a nationwide obsessional love of fish, a fetish for fish, a reverential and perhaps even spiritual approach to fish and the Tsukiji fish market in Tokyo functions, then, as a universal high temple for fish lovers. It was when other countries started developing a taste for sushi and competing successfully with Japan in buying them that most Japanese recognized, subconsciously, that Japan was no longer able to dominate the fish-eating world. Its control of the world consumption of fish weakened and its economic power faded. Now China has developed a taste for blue-finned tuna and competes with Japan to purchase them and sushi is popular all over the world, to further complicate matters.

Risking life to eat fish

Where else in the world do people risk their lives to eat fish? The Japanese eat fugu, a puffer fish, and it is estimated that every year around a number of Japanese (I have seen estimates as low as two or three people and as high as 50 people) in Japan die from eating this fish, usually because they try to eat these fish at home and have not taken the poisonous parts out of it adequately. In the special restaurants where this fish is served, the chefs have years of training, so eating this fish in these special restaurants is not seen as dangerous – although there is always the possibility that a chef in one of these fugu restaurants might make a mistake. The toxin in fugu is estimated to be 1000 times more toxic than cyanide, so even a tiny bite of a poisonous part of a fugu fish is disastrous.

Now Japan has imported American fast-food franchises and there are many McDonald's restaurants and many other kinds of ethnic restaurants to be found in all the major cities. Whether the younger generations of Japanese will carry on the passion for fish found in older generations remains to be seen.

Bento Boxes

Bento boxes with various combinations of Japanese foods are sold in a number of places in Japan such as convenience stores, supermarkets and in the basement food courts in department stores. Young children take Bento boxes full of food cooked by their mothers to school and many people who work buy them to have for lunch or dinner, to save their time and the bother of shopping for food and cooking it. What is interesting about Bento boxes is that they reflect a number of things about Japanese culture.

Photograph of Bento box

First, they reflect the enormous variety of foods that Japanese people eat. If you examine the Bento boxes in Japan, you see many different foods and combination of foods in them. It is not unusual for a Bento box to contain half a dozen or more different foods in their various compartments: chicken, vegetables, rice, noodles, sauces (in pouches) and desserts.

Second, these boxes are an example of the importance and ubiquitous nature of a highly refined Japanese aesthetic that touches many areas of Japanese life. What strikes you, when you examine a group of different Bento boxes in a store, is how beautiful the food in them looks and how elegantly the food is displayed. You can often see seaweed forming faces on hard boiled eggs, rice patties or dumplings and there are different layers of food in Bento boxes, so they often contain an element of surprise to them.

Conclusions on Japanese Icons and Daily Life

I have just dealt with a number of important aspects of Japanese culture and society. Tourists who visit Japan do not have to deal with the problems of everyday life faced by the Japanese and often come away from their visits to Japan with an unrealistic picture of life in Japan. So I have offered, in my analyses, insights into the hidden significance of any number of different icons of Japanese everyday life and culture that I believe will enrich and enhance the insights tourists gain from their visits to Japan.

In my recent visit to Japan, in May and June of 2008, I asked people I met about how they liked Japan. As one young woman said to me, when I inquired about how she was enjoying her stay, 'it's really different'. Japan *is* very different from America and western European countries and that is one of the reasons it is such an interesting country to visit. For a visit to Japan shows how important culture is and the way cultural values shape so many aspects of daily life. In the next section of this book, 'Coda', I deal with experiences I had on my recent visit to Japan.

Even an essay such as 'The Stranger' [by Georg Simmel] (updated now to guest workers) lays the groundwork for what the Bergers called the homeless mind. In some sense the great dichotomies of the classical tradition, Gemeinschaft and Gesellschaft, rural and urban, mechanical and organic, along with the evolutionary ideas in Comte, Spencer and others, suggest the emergence of a new type of person, prepared to be touring all the time, where vacation is no longer a different destination than home (e.g. staycation) and remittances are the currency that justifies going somewhere else to help people somewhere else. (Jonathan Imber, Personal Communication)

Everywhere, we find in leisure and holidays the same eager moral and idealistic pursuit of accomplishment as in the sphere of work, the same ethics of pressured performance. *No more than consumption, to which it belongs entirely, is leisure a praxis of satisfaction. Or, at least, we may that it is so only in appearance. In fact, the obsession with getting a tan, that bewildered whirl in which tourists 'do' Italy, Spain and all the art galleries, the gymnastics and nudity which are* de rigeur *under an obligatory sun and, most important of all, the smiles and unfailing* joie de vivre *all attest to the fact that the holiday-maker conforms in every detail to the principles of duty, sacrifice and asceticism ... The increasingly marked tendency towards the physical concentration of tourists and holiday-makers – which stands in formal contradiction to the declared motive or pursuing freedom and autonomy – obeys the same principle of constraint which is homologous with that experienced in work.* (Jean Baudrillard, The Consumer Society: Myths and Structures)

Chapter 5
Tourism and Cultural Change in Japan

We have to make a distinction between cultural change and social change. Social change, as I understand the term, focuses attention on changes to societal institutions such as marriage, education, religion and the political order. Cultural change, on the other hand, involves changes to values, beliefs and attitudes that inform a culture. As Stuart Hall points out, culture is now seen semiotically, in terms of the shared meanings of practices. He writes in *Cultural Representations and Signifying Practices*:

> What has been called the 'cultural turn' in the social and human sciences, especially in cultural studies and the sociology of culture, has tended to emphasize the importance of *meaning* to the definition of culture. Culture, it is argued, is not so much a set of *things* – novels and paintings of TV programmes and comics – as a process, a set of *practices*. Primarily, culture is concerned with the production and exchange of meanings – the 'giving and taking of meaning' – between the members of a society or group ... The emphasis on cultural practices is important. Things 'in themselves' rarely if ever have any one, single, fixed and unchanging meaning. (Hall, 1997: 2)

Hall's notion of culture as semiotic in nature is one that informs both this book and its interpretations of various aspects of Japanese culture.

Cultural change and social and political change are inter-related and it is difficult to say whether social change leads to cultural change or the reverse. Daniel Patrick Moynihan has suggested an answer to this dilemma:

> The central conservative truth is that is culture, not politics, that determines the success of a society. The central liberal truth is that politics can change a culture and save it from itself. (http://Fletcher.

Tufts.edu/cci) (The Cultural Change Institute at the Fletcher School of Diplomacy, Tufts University)

This analysis will focus on cultural change, after a brief discussion of social change and the ideas of three of the most important classical sociologists. They were concerned primarily with social change. Jonathan Imber, a sociologist at Wellesley College, suggests, in the quotation at the beginning of this chapter, that 'the homeless mind' and the phenomena connected to it, such as postmodernism, are leading to a new kind of person – a perennial tourist. For these people, tourism becomes a vocation, not an interruption from everyday life. As Baudrillard suggests, in his book on consumer culture, tourism has now become a kind of work, with imperatives similar to those in the workplace.

Classical Theories of Social Change

In the book *Core Sociological Dichotomies*, Fran Tonkiss has a chapter titled 'Continuity/Change', which discusses the importance of theories of social change to sociologists. Tonkiss writes:

> The analysis of how and why societies change is one of the most basic and the most difficult concerns for sociology. As a discipline, classical sociology set itself the task of explaining the emergent form of modern society. Thinkers such as Comte, Marx, Durkheim and Weber sought in different ways to capture the specific character of the *modern*, and suggested how this might be distinguished from *traditional* ways of life. (Tonkiss, 1998: 35)

We see, then, that the matter of social and cultural change has been a preoccupation of social scientists for many years. Cultural change is also a subject of considerable importance to tourism scholars and there is a journal, the *Journal of Tourism and Cultural Change*, published by Routledge, devoted to that subject.

The chart below lists terms used by Durkheim, Toennnies and Weber, three important classical sociologists, to describe social change.

Sociologist	*From*	*To*
Durkheim	Mechanical solidarity	Organic solidarity
Toennies	Gemeinschaft	Gesellschaft
Weber	Charisma	Rationalization

For Durkheim, mechanical solidarity is dominant when people have strong ties between one another and no major differences among themselves, while organic solidarity prevails when ties between people are weak and commitment to one another is lacking. Organic solidarity is connected to the division of labour in these societies. In organic societies (the terms Durkheim used are somewhat misleading), relationships are partial, with increased anomie or normlessness, but, on the other hand, there are also increased opportunities for self-development.

Toennies argued that there are two kinds of societies – those characterized by Gemeinschaft, where there are strong and enduring relationships among people and Gesellschaft, and where relationships among people are weak and partial. We find Gemeinschaft in families and Gesellschaft in jobs and corporations. What Toennies argued is that modern societies have moved from ones that could be characterized as Gemeinschaft in nature to ones characterized by Gesellschaft.

Max Weber's analysis of social change centred on the change from revolutionary charismatic authorities, who lead by virtue of their powerful personalities to rationalized or rational–legal authorities. The problem with charismatic movements is that they are inherently unstable, for when charismatic leaders die, they don't leave anyone to replace them.

In a very general way, we can say that tourism represents an attempt to escape, at least for a short while, from the bureaucratic, rational, mechanical and organic societies in which tourists live to earlier stages when different and more humane kinds of relationships existed between people. Georg Simmel writes, in his essay 'The Adventure', about 'dropping out of the continuity of life' for a short period of time and escaping from everyday life's 'continuous thread'. What he writes about adventures applies very directly to tourism and the kinds of experiences tourists seek and often have:

> Something becomes an adventure only by virtue of two conditions: that it itself is a specific organization of some significant meaning with a beginning and an end; and that, despite its accidental nature, its extra-territoriality with respect to the continuity of life, it nevertheless connects with the character and identity of the bearer of that life – that it does so in the widest sense, transcending, by a mysterious necessity, life's more narrowly rational aspects. (Simmel, 1997: 222)

As tourism has evolved and become the largest industry in the world, many tourism scholars, from a variety of disciplines, have become interested in the matter of social and cultural change. This book is part of a series of volumes devoted to the relationship between tourism and cultural change and demonstrates the importance of this subject to tourism scholars in different disciplines.

Kinds of Tourists and Cultural Change

When discussing tourism and change in Japan, we have to distinguish between Japanese tourists visiting different parts of Japan and tourists from other countries who visit Japan. It is reasonable to suggest that foreign tourists, who may have different values and beliefs systems, and different expectations of Japanese culture, will have a greater impact on Japanese cultural change than Japanese tourists. Japanese tourists visiting Japan generally do not bring major differences in their cultural beliefs to the places they visit while foreign tourists do.

Let us hypothesize that tourists from first-world countries who visit so-called undeveloped or under-developed third-world countries can have a more profound impact and generate more cultural change in these countries than they do in first-world countries. That is because third-world cultures are generally more willing to make changes in their social and cultural practices to accommodate foreign tourists in order to gain needed revenue. As I point out later in this chapter, we should not over-estimate the impact of first-world countries on third-world ones, for they have ways of resisting or moderating the kind of cultural change one might expect from tourism. Inhabitants of third-world countries may, in some cases, feel resentment and a sense of inferiority towards more affluent foreign tourists. The inhabitants of these countries often want to have the same quality of life and possessions that tourists from richer countries have, a phenomenon known as 'the demonstration effect'.

Japan is a first-world country with a very distinctive culture that developed the way it did, in part, because of Japan's long isolation from the rest of the world. It has a very high standard of living and the Japanese are, generally speaking, affluent. Tourists from other countries who come to Japan do not generate a 'demonstration effect' in tourist industry workers with whom they interact because the Japanese are so affluent. Instead, foreign visitors to Japan may experience a reverse 'demonstration effect' themselves because of the prices of things in Japan and may feel poor when compared to the Japanese people. It is a bit overwhelming for foreign tourists to see a $50 melon in the food sections of department stores.

The same kind of reversal involves the 'tourist gaze', which theorizes that tourists visiting foreign countries 'gaze' upon landscapes and other photo opportunities and on the inhabitants of these countries from a position of superiority and dominance. In Japan, one might argue that foreign tourists are gazed upon by the Japanese – what we might call the gaze from local inhabitants – who do not exhibit a sense of inferiority but the reverse, given Japan's affluence and economic power.

Sources of Cultural Change

In addition to the theories of classical sociologists about social change, there are many competing and sometimes conflicting explanations of what generates cultural change. We may ask ourselves a number of questions about the causes of cultural change. Is it essentially caused by economic factors? Is it the result of changes in the political order? What role do wars and military conquests play in shaping cultural change? Do popular culture and the mass media play important roles in shaping cultural change? What role do technologies play in cultural change? Are large global cultural movements, such as the development of postmodern societies, behind cultural change? We can suggest that all of these factors play a role in cultural change.

Tourism, whatever else it may be, can be seen as a kind of consumption. People travel because they value experiences and the psychological and emotional benefits they gain from visiting other sites in their own country or other countries. But travel is often expensive. Most citizens of affluent countries, such as France, Italy, the United States, Japan and England, have enough disposable income to travel and are willing to use their financial resources to do so. If there is a recession, people are poorer and even wealthy people feel poorer, and this affects their travel plans. As a result of the recession of 2009, for example, many Americans changed their travel plans and took 'staycations' or ended up taking less expensive foreign trips. The same applies to citizens of other countries. In addition, the swine flu epidemic led many tourists to abandon plans for visits to foreign countries and stick closer to home.

So, the economy plays an important role in tourism. When the economic situation is good and people feel well off, they are inclined to travel in greater numbers, which means more tourists visit foreign countries and their impact is, collectively speaking, greater. According to Marius B. Jansen, one of the co-authors of *The Japanese Today: Change and Continuity*, the success of the Japanese economy in the early 1990s led to something like 40,000 young Japanese studying in the United States, where they could gain insights into American culture. They were not tourists in the conventional sense of the term, but foreign students often travel widely in America, so these students spent part of their time as tourists. When these students returned to Japan, they brought with them an understanding of American culture and a different sensibility.

The subtitle of *The Japanese Today* suggests a pattern that applies to all cultures: on the one hand, there is continuity and an attachment to the 'old' ways and on the other, there is continual change – sometimes evolutionary and sometimes revolutionary – and a desire for new kinds of cultural practices. The Japanese also travel abroad in great numbers. It is reasonable to assume that their visits to foreign countries expose them to different cultural arrangements that may cause them to question certain aspects of Japanese culture and to adopt certain practices and behaviours found in the countries they have visited.

Japanese tourists, as Shinji Yamashita points out in *Bali and Beyond*, work very hard and are wonderful examples of the way the 'work' ethic is often reflected in tourism. Baudrillard's discussion of tourism as homologous with work is very accurate when it comes to the behaviour of Japanese tourists in Bali, but also of Japanese tourists in other countries and, to a degree, tourists everywhere. But not all tourists want to 'do' six European countries in a 10-day trip and some tourists actually go to beaches and nature reserves to relax.

Foreign tourists also often play a role in modifying or changing the behaviour of political regimes in a society. Countries with repressive political regimes often find that they need to moderate their behaviour lest they cause problems for the tourism industries in their countries, often an important source of revenues. What happened in China during the Olympics is a good example of the way in which tourism influences governmental behaviour, even though the impact of the Olympics upon the Chinese government does not seem to be long-lasting.

Once a regime starts making changes to accommodate foreign visitors, it is difficult to return to the old order. So tourists, in many cases, play a role in lessening the grip of authoritarian governments and moving them to provide things that foreign tourists want. For example, tourism requires a good infrastructure to facilitate travel in a country; tourism exerts pressure on governments to allow writers, creative artists, musicians, dancers and playwrighters more freedom, and tourism leads to governments preserving historical monuments, parks and nature reserves for Ecotourists.

We also have to consider the influence of the mass media and popular culture on all cultures. Media scholars often use the term 'media imperialism' to deal with the way in which films, television shows, songs, music videos, video games and other forms of first-world media countries affect third-world cultures. This 'Coca-Colonization' (or 'McDonaldization' as it is sometimes called) is not propaganda and the capitalist messages found in the media are not inserted consciously into the mass-mediated texts. Instead, the bourgeois values found in these texts reflect the values and beliefs of the writers and makers of these texts.

We must not underestimate the impact of mass-mediated pop culture on other countries, even Japan (and the impact of Japanese pop culture on other countries). Japan is considered one of the most important media imperialist countries, thanks to its rock musicians, anime, manga and video games and, at one time, its films. To this mix we must now add new technologies, such as cell phones and MP3 players and social media such as Facebook and Twitter and communication programmes such as Skype. The world is now, as McLuhan put it, a 'global village' and in this village, new ideas and ways of behaving evolve and spread rapidly.

We can also think of tourism as a diluted form of cultural imperialism in that tourists indirectly impose, to varying degrees, their values, beliefs and desires, on the countries they visit. Tourists want to be comfortable, want to see 'authentic' dances, musical exhibitions and rituals (although this matter of a search for authenticity is debated by tourism scholars), and have other desires and needs that have an impact on the countries they visit. Some scholars, such as Lévi-Strauss, have suggested that cultural change is leading to the development of a global 'monoculture' in which differences among cultures are becoming so minimal that tourism in no longer worthwhile. He laments in *Tristes Tropiques*:

> There was a time when travel confronted the traveller with civilizations radically different from his own. It was their strangeness, above all, which impressed him. But these opportunities have been getting rarer and rarer for a very long time. Be it in India or in America, the traveller of our days finds things more familiar than he will admit. (Lévi-Strauss, 1970: 90)

For Levi-Strauss, the rise of a global monoculture means that there are no significant differences between cultures, so travelling to them is not worthwhile. That would suggest the inevitable development of a kind of post-tourism postmodern world.

On the other hand, sociologist Ning Wang gives us reason for optimism. He writes in *Tourism and Modernity* that globalization has not destroyed distinctive cultures:

> Globalization does not eradicate difference, variety, and diversity. Historically, the Enlightenment thinkers insisted that globalization, as the extension of Western order, reason, values, and civilization to the rest of the world, should lead to the universalization, homogenization,

and Westernization of the world. History has proved that this was not only a justification for colonialism, but also a utopia. In reality, even if globalization has indeed led to what Hannerz (1987) calls 'cultural creolization', is has not eradicated difference. The world today is one of difference, diversity, and pluralism rather than sameness. (Wang, 2000: 133)

Despite the fact that there are many American fast-food companies in foreign countries, they still retain their distinctive cultural qualities. The thousands of KFC and McDonald's restaurants in China and Japan have not had profound effects on Chinese or Japanese culture, but these restaurants and other fast-food restaurants are contributing to the growing obesity problems in both countries.

The mass media probably have had a disproportionate impact on Japanese youth. Japanese youth are an enigma to older Japanese and have rejected many of the beliefs and values of earlier generations. As Jansen writes:

What of the young? Japanese, like other people, profess great difficulty in understanding the values and attitudes of their juniors. There is now a generation of young people that seems to its elders unappreciative of the enormous effort that has gone into making Japan what it is, that takes material things for granted, that wants vacation and relaxation time as much as it does work, and that wants that work to be interesting as well as properly compensated. (Jansen, 1994: 441)

In the years since 1994, Japanese youth has become more materialistic and more alienated and distanced from traditional Japanese values, as exemplified by the hikikomori, punks and parasite children found in that country.

Finally, we must add what might be described as global cultural changes such as the rise and triumph of postmodern societies, of which Japan is an exemplar. The impact of postmodernism on Japanese culture was discussed earlier in the book. Postmodernists argue that around 1960 there was a radical change in cultures as the old traditionalist and modernist cultures and societies were replaced by postmodern ones. These postmodern societies are characterized by the increased importance of simulations, the growth of media, a lack of concern about 'original' works of art, the breakdown of distinctions between elite culture and popular culture and the development of consumer cultures.

In postmodern societies, the pastiche is the quintessential visual art form and the shuffle in MP3 players is its audio analogue. And, relative to this point – one might argue that postmodernism does not break down the difference between different cultures but enables an eclectic lifestyle, as the Lyotard passage quoted earlier in the book suggests. Some theorists argue that postmodernism amalgamates all cultures into one postmodern monoculture, but that seems to me to be a contradiction in terms.

These different perspectives on cultural change might suggest that third-world native cultures have no chance to resist them, but this is not correct. One reason people over-estimate the impact of first-world countries on third-world or traditional cultures is that it is assumed that these cultures were static and rigid. That is generally not the case, for even traditional societies evolve continually, and find ways to assimilate different cultures and yet maintain, to varying degrees, their own distinctive cultures.

Consider, for example, the case of Thailand. As Erik H. Cohen writes in his book *The Commercialized Crafts of Thailand: Hill Tribes and Lowland Villages*:

> It should be noted indeed that even in the past most Third and Fourth world people were not isolated from external influences. Their arts and crafts were throughout history influenced by the styles, designs, materials and techniques of other cultures and societies. (Cohen, 2000: 5)

If members of so-called 'primitive' or traditional societies can find ways of accommodating cultural changes, then certainly advanced countries such as Japan can do so as well.

Tourism's Cultural Impact on Japan

We start this discussion with the recognition that there are continual changes in the cultures of all countries. Change is a constant. The pace of change is another matter. Japan does not have as many tourists as Thailand or China or many other countries. The tourist authorities in Japan are still trying to get 10 million foreign tourists to visit Japan in a given year. So there are not huge numbers of foreign tourists who come to Japan the way they go to France and Spain, for example.

But there was one experience that is somewhat analogous to having a flood of tourists visiting Japan, namely the American occupation of Japan, in the years after the Second World War. In *Tokyo Rising: The City Since the Great Earthquake*, Edward Seidensticker writes:

> On August 15, for the first time in the history of the land, the Emperor made a radio broadcast. He announced acceptance of the Potsdam Declaration. (Seidensticker, 1991: 145)

We might consider this a pivotal moment in Japanese history and an example of the impact that the American triumph in Second World War had on Japanese culture and society. Even the emperor was forced to change his ways, and in present-day Japan, the emperor while still loved and respected, is no longer seen as a living god.

Although occupying troops are not tourists in the conventional sense, if we adapt Simmel's theories and think of tourists and American soldiers as 'strangers', we can assume that the Americans stationed in Japan generated or accelerated significant changes in Japanese culture. The American military's change to Japan's constitution had major ramifications on Japanese culture and helped move it politically and socially into being more modern and more democratic. The American military also encouraged the development of baseball in Japan, where it has become a very important spectator sport. As might be expected, the Japanese have made certain adjustments, tied to their culture, on how the game is played.

The Place of this Book in the Cultural Tourism Series

The books in this series on tourism and cultural change deal with topics dealt with in *Tourism in Japan: An Ethno-Semiotic Analysis*, namely the relationship that exists between tourism and the development of a sense of identity, the dislocations caused by economic upheavals, wars and natural disasters, and the distinctive qualities found in a given culture. Some of the books in this series, such as Michael Cronin and Barbara O'Connor's *Irish Tourism* and Erik H. Cohen's *Youth Tourism in Israel*, focus on particular countries. Others, such as *Tourism, Globalization and Cultural Change*, deal with tourism in terms of topics such as globalization, identity, the types and motivations of tourists and the impact of tourism on the beliefs and values of people in different cultures.

Readers of *Tourism in Japan: An Ethno-Semiotic Analysis* will find that it offers semiotically informed interpretations of what can be described as 'iconic' aspects of Japanese culture and society and, in particular, analyses of some of the developments and changes that have taken place in recent years that are profoundly affecting Japanese culture.

Which Japan? Male manager dominated middle-class Japan? ... Is it urban Japan or rural Japan, the Japan of small nuclear families or of the single young woman? Is there one Japanese society? ... We cannot ignore the common assumption that Japan the nation and Japanese society are one single thing ... If asked, most Westerners probably could outline what [the dominant] image of Japan is: a homogenous society, where hierarchy and formality continue to be important. A country where men still are dominant and all work for large companies as modern 'samurai' businessman. Japanese women are held to be gentle, submissive and beautiful, and yet also appear in the foreign media as pushy mothers obsessed with their children's education. Japanese children, by extension, must be miserable automatons who do nothing but study all day and half the night. Japanese society is portrayed as one where esthetics and harmony are highly valued, and yet feudal violence lives on in the guise of the yakusa [yakuza] *(gangsters). In short, images of this modern state still depict it as a place of contradictions, difficult to understand for any outside naïve enough to try. Matters are not helped by the fact that the Japanese themselves hold these images up as valid representations of their own society.* (Martinez, 1998)

Chapter 6

Coda: A Return to Japan

My wife Phyllis and I left San Francisco on an 11:30 am flight on United Airlines for Tokyo. We had been to Japan some 20 years before and wondered what we would find on our new visit. We arrived in Narita airport on 15 May in the afternoon. We took a train from Narita to Ueno Station and then a subway to Asakusa. That cost around 1000 yen for each of us. When we got out at the Asakusa station, on the Ginza line, we were faced with a problem: which exit should we take? I asked a woman who was near us, showing her a map of the Asakusa area, but she did not know English. She asked some people around her whether anyone in the station knew English.

Our First Encounters with Helpful Japanese Persons

A woman who did speak English saw us and came running over to help us. I explained to her that we were trying to figure out which exit to take to get to the Toyoko Inn that we had booked. There are two Toyoko Inns in the Asakusa section of Tokyo and we had booked a room in one called the Asakusa Senzoku.

'Let me help you', she said. She took a small bag I had on top of my suitcase and led my wife and me to an exit – about a three-minute walk – and then she carried my bag up the stairs in the station until we got to the pavement. She told us which direction to go to find our hotel, welcomed us to Japan and returned to the station. As we were walking, an elderly man riding a bicycle stopped near us. 'How may I help you'? he asked. I told him I was looking for the Toyoko Inn's Asakusa Senzoku hotel and he got off his bike and walked with us until we had reached a corner, crossed the street and were on the right street, heading towards the hotel. 'You can't miss it now', he said, and then went riding off.

One thing that surprised me about Tokyo was the number of people riding bicycles – generally on the pavements. You see large number of bicycles in front of supermarkets and McDonalds's all through Japan and when you walk in Japan, you always have to watch out for bike riders. During the course of our visit in Japan we were amazed at how kind Japanese people were to us and how they often went out of their way to help us find temples or other places we wanted to visit.

The Sanja Matsuri Festival in Asakusa

As I explained earlier, in my discussion of the Sanja Matsuri festival, it turned out that our visit to Asakusa was timed perfectly, for there was a gigantic three-day Sanja Matsuri festival in Asakusa that drew millions of people to watch groups of 70 or 80 Japanese men and women carry large portable shrines (Mikashi) that weighed around 2000 pounds through the streets. So our return to Japan got off to an exciting start.

Members of a parade in Asakusa Sanja Matsuri festival

Booking our stays with the Toyoko Inns was an ordeal. The company has a website but it is extremely difficult to use. I tried calling the Senzoku

hotel in Asakusa but the clerk who answered the phone when I called did
not speak English. Finally, I located the phone number for the corporation's
information centre [011 813 5714 4589] and called it. I found someone with
limited English who was able to make reservations for me in Asakusa and
in Kanazawa. I decided to stay in a different hotel in Kyoto, The Palace Side
Hotel, which offered discounts for stays of six nights or more.

One added benefit of the Toyoko Inns is that they serve a modest breakfast of coffee or tea, rice cakes and miso soup. When we went to the dining
room area, the Japanese women who were preparing the rice cakes and
soup always greeted us and smiled. All of our hotels in Japan had small
refrigerators, so you can keep milk and other foods in them and self-cater
your breakfasts by purchasing sweet rolls or bread and jam at supermarkets. You can also get good take out food at supermarkets and food stalls
in the basements of department stores if you get tired of the Japanese food
sold in all the small restaurants that are everywhere in Japan.

Plastic food display

They generally have a collection of plastic models of the dinners they
serve, with the price of each dinner shown near it. Most of the meals in
these small restaurants are between $4 and $10, depending on what you
order. Our first lunch cost around $8 each and consisted of a bowl of rice

with tempura, a small plate with pickles and a large bowl of soup with noodles in it. It was quite delicious.

Asakusa is one of the more charming areas of Tokyo and we enjoyed walking around different parts of Asakusa and taking part in the festivities connected with Sanja Matsuri. We had been to other parts of Tokyo on a previous visit, so we stayed in Asakusa, for the most part, although we did take a river cruise from Asakusa to an area near the huge Tokyo fish market. We walked down to see what the fish market area looked like and then went looking for a subway station.

Lost in the Shimbashi Subway Station

We got lost looking for a subway near the fish market. A sign near the place we got off the river cruise pointed to a subway but we could not see one anywhere. We were helped by a young Japanese man, who, by chance was heading for the subway station. Fortunately, he spoke English. 'I'm going to the subway station', he said. 'Please follow me'. The Shimbashi subway station is really gigantic and it took us 10 or 15 min, asking for help in many different stores in the station, to find our way to the Ginza line, which would take us back to Asakusa. Subway stations in Japan can be enormous, full of stores and restaurants, and the Shimbashi station is very large, so we wandered around for a long time before we saw any signs indicating the way to the Ginza line.

Expect To Be Lost Many Times in Japan

If you are going to travel in Japan on your own, you have to realize that there will be any number of times when you will be lost and will need help. What complicates matters is that relatively few Japanese speak English, although many of them have studied it for years. The problem is they do not learn conversational English and so cannot help you. Time and time again were amazed at how helpful the Japanese were and how they would go out of their way and spend five minutes or so to lead you to streets where you could find some temple you were looking for. I have never been in a country where the people were so helpful to tourists.

In some cases, we would show a map with a location written in Japanese to a person who did not know English, but who spent a few minutes, talking in Japanese to us, assuming that somehow we would figure out what they were saying. These encounters generally ended up with our helpers pointing with their hands as if to say 'go this way down this street, then go that way'. It is important that you carry some document with the place you wish to go written in Japanese. Eventually, you will find someone who speaks English who can help you.

We spent our last day in Tokyo in Ueno, which is near Asakusa. We took advantage of a free tour offered by the local tourism board in Ueno and had a two-hour tour through Ueno with a retired businessman who was extremely interesting. A young German woman took the tour with us. She was teaching German in Japan and had been there for several months. 'It's hard on me because I'm a vegetarian', she said. 'I live on ice cream'. In the course of our visit to Japan, I was to develop a fondness for ice cream, especially the 100-yen ice cream cones sold at McDonald's, one of the best (and few) bargains in Japan. Occasionally, when we were rushed, we also enjoyed the 100-yen hamburgers at McDonald's.

Travelling by Long-Distance Buses in Japan

I went to a tourism agency in Asakusa and purchased bus tickets to take us from Tokyo to Takayama, our next destination. For some reason it took about 20 minutes for us to get the tickets. We decided to go to Takayama, Kanazawa and Kyoto by bus, so we could see more of the country and also save money. The bus from Tokyo to Takayama cost around $65, the bus from Takayama to Kanazawa cost around $33 and the bus from Kanazawa to Kyoto cost around $40 per person. This totalled around $150 per person for bus tickets, which was a great deal less than travelling by train. A seven-day rail pass in Japan costs around $280 and a 14-day rail pass costs around $450, so it was much less expensive travelling by bus.

We also stopped at a number of rest stops on each trip and that gave me a chance to see what these rests stops were like. The prices for meals in the rest stops were no different from restaurants in Japanese cities, but our stops were so brief that it was not possible to have lunch. If you are not in a great hurry, I would recommend travelling by bus in Japan. We spent two days in Takayama and Kanazawa and 13 nights in Kyoto, which we used as a base to visit cities such as Nara and Osaka.

In Tokyo, we had our bus tickets but we faced the problem of finding the bus station, which is near the gigantic Shinjuku subway station. I felt a considerable amount of anxiety about finding the right exit from Shinjuku and then finding the bus station. We were given detailed information by the clerks at our hotel, and knew that we should take the west exit from Shinjuku to get to the bus station. I had also seen where the bus station was on a map of the area, yet when we exited the Shinjuko station we did not have the slightest idea of how to get to the bus station. We found the station by asking people how to get to it and finally, after asking three or four people, to our great relief, we arrived in the station about 20 minutes before it was to leave. Our bus was at 9:00 am. If we missed it, we would have to hang around for a few hours until the next bus left for Takayama, so we felt a bit of pressure.

The bus ride to Takayama took six hours, but it was broken up with a couple of stops at rest stations. It was quite a lovely trip, as a matter of fact, and gave us the chance to see a good deal of Japan. Takayama is located in the hills and so our bus kept climbing. The Toyoko chain does not have a hotel in Takayama so I booked a hotel – The Takayama Central – using the internet, with a Japanese travel agency. The hotel cost around $80 a night and we were there for two nights. It was not as nice as the Toyoko Inn, but it was conveniently located, perhaps a three-minute walk from the bus station. I found there were many hotels in the city that had free rooms so even if we had not booked ahead, we could have got a room.

Takayama Adventures

Takayama has a number of tourist attractions, such as some very old merchant houses, a positively stunning building from 'old' Japan, the Takayama – Jin'ya, [jinja] and the Hida Folk Village, which is a collection of old houses, many with thatched roofs, that give you an idea of how many Japanese in rural areas lived many years ago. It rained lightly, off and on, all day long, but we had brought umbrellas and were not too bothered by the rain.

When we were on the street with the old merchant houses, a group of Americans with Japanese 'hosts' were wandering around. The Americans were from Denver and one of the Americans was, it turned out, the mayor of Denver. Denver is a sister city of Takayama and the mayor and some officials from the city were on a visit. We then went to the Takayama Jinja, which is a superb example of Japanese minimalism. It was a government building and its spatiality and simplicity were absolutely stunning. In the afternoon we went to the Hida Folk Village, and bumped into the mayor's group again. We chatted with one of the Americans who turned out, I discovered later, to be the mayor.

Takayama is quite small and you can visit most of it on foot. You need to take a bus to the Hida Folk Village. Parts of Takayama are very touristy and as I walked along one of the streets I felt I could have been in Sausalito or any one of a number of other tourist meccas. The kinds of shops and the designs of the shops and their signs are pretty standard for tourist areas everywhere. There is, I suggest, a kind of universal tourist aesthetic found on upscale shopping streets everywhere.

Jin'Ya Feudal Era Hall in Takayama

Thatched roof house in tourist village near Takayama

A number of tours of Japan, some of which I described earlier, visit Takayama, Kanazawa and Kyoto and we were following the route. We spent an afternoon and the next day seeing the sights in Takayama and then we boarded a bus for Kanazawa.

Kanazawa

Kanazawa is a large city of around 500,000 people, so we needed to take a bus from the bus station/railway station to our hotel there, the Toyoko Inn's Kanazawa Korinbo. It is a large, modern building, located near some department stores and within walking distance of Kanazawa's two major attractions – its castle and its famous garden, considered one of the three best Japanese gardens in Japan.

Because we arrived at the Kanazawa Korinbo around one o'clock, we had to leave our bags in the lobby. One of the clerks brought our bags into a holding area and we wandered off to look around the area and visit the castle and the garden. Many hotels in Japan do not allow guests to register before two o'clock in the afternoon but the Toyoko Inn's do not allow guests to go to their rooms before four o'clock.

Somehow we got lost again and ended up at the Kanazawa-jo castle instead of the gardens. The Kanazawa castle is an extraordinary building, which was restored in recent years at a cost of 4 billion yen. It has enormous wooden beams that are ingeniously fitted together and takes around 30 minutes to see. At various places there are videos showing how the building was restored. It is one of the more interesting castles that we visited while in Japan.

The Kenroku-en garden is a short walk from the castle. It is very large and was crowded with people – mostly Japanese tourists. In the course of our travels in Japan, we saw relatively few tourists from the United States or western Europe. Most of the tourists in Japan are Japanese or from other nearby Asian countries. We spent around an hour walking through the garden, which has many beautiful areas in it – although I would say that I enjoyed other, smaller gardens in Kyoto temples more than this garden, perhaps because they were more manageable.

We had done a great deal of walking that afternoon and were very tired when we returned to our hotel. The Toyoko Inns do not carry international television channels, so I contented myself with watching women's volleyball – the only programme on television that I did not need Japanese to appreciate. I was to spend quite a few evenings in Japan watching the Japanese women's volleyball team play other teams before we arrived in Kyoto, where our hotel had both BBC-TV and CNN-TV.

Kanazawa castle interior

Last Day in Kanazawa

On our last day in Kanazawa, we went to the Myoryu-ji temple and had a guided tour, in Japanese. Every visitor to the temple must go on a guided tour. We were given a booklet in English that explained some of the things we saw – mostly secret passages and hiding places that enabled those in the temple to kill, hide from or escape from enemies who might attack the temple. During this tour we tagged along with a group of school children who were visiting the temple. We were to spend the rest of our stay in Japan surrounded by hundreds and hundreds of school children, in various uniforms, who were on cultural visits. The temple was not that interesting to me except as an example of the paranoia that existed and was reflected in the temple's architecture. We also spent some time in a department store's food court, which turned out to be a wonderful experience.

More on Food Courts in Department Stores

In Kanazawa, we had a great time at the food court in the basement of the Daiwa department store – a paradise for food lovers. These food courts are filled with all kinds of delicious foods and some foods – fish eggs, kinds of fish and strange vegetables – that are quite foreign to Americans. At this store the clerk in the fish egg section spent 10 minutes giving us different samples of fish eggs and strange fish parts, relishing our astonishment at some of the foods he was offering. He spoke English and described the foods we were sampling.

Department store food court

The food court also had some very expensive melons that Japanese give to one another as gifts, a French bakery, and rows and rows of other foods – most of which could be sampled. Aside from the fish we ate, we were given pot stickers (delicious) and sampled any number of other kinds of pastries and other foods. Most of the food counters have little trays with samples that you eat with toothpicks and the clerks behind the counters often offer other foods. The cost melons is one of the things that make people in foreign countries feel that Japan is so expensive.

The ambience of those food courts is paradisical for food lovers and, as I pointed out earlier in this book, the food courts account for a significant amount of the profits at the big department stores. The food courts reminded me of the feeling you get in Whole Foods stores, but the food courts in Japanese supermarkets are better and more lavish, with more food at even higher prices than Whole Foods. In the department stores, there were large displays of fruits and vegetables – unlike what you find in most Japanese supermarkets.

An Aside on Japanese Supermarkets

During our visit to Japan, we also went to some supermarkets and were astonished to find that some of them were full of foods that we could not recognize. We did not have the slightest idea of what these foods were, which reflects the difference between American food preferences and Japanese ones. Whereas American supermarkets have huge displays of vegetables and fruits, in the Japanese supermarkets there were relatively few fruits and vegetables.

The bread sections of supermarkets were quite interesting. In one supermarket that we went to in Kyoto, the same size loaf of bread was sold in packages with five slices, six slices, eight slices and ten slices. The Japanese, it seems, like thick slices of toast – slices twice as thick as we get in American bread. The bread was balloon white bread – which I had not eaten for years. There were some other breads and there were bakeries around in most cities that sold French bread, so it is possible to eat decent bread in Japan. The train station in Kanazawa had a German bakery with some rye breads and wonderful pastries.

On to Kyoto

The next morning we caught a bus to the bus station, which was right next to the train station, and hopped on the 10 o'clock bus to Kyoto. The trip from Kanazawa to Kyoto took a bit more than three hours. We had been in Japan for eight nights and would be spending 13 nights in Kyoto, at the Palace Side Hotel. On the bus, sitting behind us, was a young man from America who was teaching English in Japan. He told us he was part of a programme, now being discontinued, that paid for native English speakers to teach in Japan.

'How do you like it'? I asked.

'It's very difficult', he replied. 'I'm not in a conventional school. Our students don't wear uniforms. The school is for dropouts, for kids who have been kicked out of regular schools, for kids who have been bullied in schools, and for autistic kids. They are all dumped together and it doesn't work'.

'That's interesting', I said. 'I'd always been under the impression that the Japanese school system was excellent'.

'I'd say it's a mess', he answered. 'They keep forming commissions to change the system but they never made any important changes'.

We chatted for a while longer and he got off at a stop before the main bus station in Kyoto. We went to the information office on the second floor of the railway station, where the bus let us off, and got lots of maps and other tourist material. A clerk there also called the Palace Office and straightened out a problem we had with booking a tour of the Palace grounds. We bought tickets on the subway for a ride to the Marutamachi station, four stops away, got off, took the exit suggested by the Palace Side to get there – exit number two, and walked a few blocks to the Palace Side Hotel.

It had the advantage of offering reduced rates for stays of six nights or longer and larger rooms than those in the Toyoko Inns. Our room had a double bed, a small sofa, a desk and chair, and a small table. It had a small refrigerator and a tea maker. We were to use the table for meals. The Palace Side Hotel also has a kitchen on the second floor – with stoves, a microwave, a toaster and cups and dishes – and I was to use it to make our breakfasts and some other meals: toast in the morning, which we had with tea. I also generally had milk and cereal for breakfast. We had our own breakfasts instead of those offered by the hotel, which cost 1200 yen per person. There was a Fresco supermarket a couple of blocks from the hotel, where I purchased bread, milk and other foods when we were self-catering.

My wife had made very detailed plans for our stay in Kyoto, which we were using as a home base to visit a number of wonderful temples and, later on, Nara and Himeji. Kyoto has some absolutely spectacular temples. These temples are actually compounds with many buildings and usually with impressive gates, so when you visit these temples, you can also look at a number of other buildings and often enjoy their gardens. In Kyoto you can purchase bus passes for 500 yen that allow you to take as many buses as you want for that day. So just about every morning, I would purchase two all-day bus passes at our hotel and then we would be off to visit important temples and other sites of interest.

The first day of our sightseeing it drizzled, off and all, all day. My wife had mapped out an ambitious programme of visiting temples 'near' one another, and I would estimate that we walked four or five miles going from one temple to another, generally surrounded by hundreds and hundreds of school children at every temple. We were to spend the next five days visiting temples and other sites of interest. Every night we would fall asleep absolutely exhausted from our exertions. Being a tourist is hard work, even under the most optimal circumstances. Most of the time the weather was fine and so we were able to visit a number of more important temples in Kyoto. I would say that my favourite temple was Ryoan-ji, the one with the famous Zen rock garden and another superb garden on its grounds as well, but there were many others that were quite remarkable. In Kyoto, the main tourist attractions are shrines, temples and gardens. We could always tell that we were getting near a temple or other tourist site when we saw legions of uniformed school children tramping around.

Japanese school children

Teaching Japanese Students about American Humour

Goh Abe, a Japanese professor, had arranged to interview me for an article on my writings on humour, so we had a day off on Thursday, 29 May. My wife and I were so tired that we could not have done any sightseeing that day. Goh came and we spent a couple of hours in a coffee shop talking about my work on humour. He had a number of questions to ask me about my theories and he recorded our entire conversation. On the next day, May 30, my wife and I went to Osaka where I was to give a lecture on American visual humour and then lead a workshop on deconstructing jokes. Goh Abe had contacted a professor at Kinki University, Sachiko Kitazume, who was hosting me. I had met them both at a humour conference in Oakland, California, around 10 years earlier.

I had a bit of anxiety about finding a place to meet her so I chose a hotel that was near the train station in Osaka. My wife and I went to see the castle in Osaka (not worth the bother, I would say) and then hopped on the subway and arrived at the Hotel Gran Via a few minutes before one o'clock, when we were to meet. I had written to Sachiko and said we would wait for her in front of the hotel. For some reason, the Gran Via had fenced off the space that cars might use to pull up to the hotel. Around ten after one, I started getting worried. A young Japanese woman who had observed us came over and asked if she could help us. I told her that a friend was coming to pick us up and everything was fine, so she left. Ten minutes later she returned. 'I'm still worried about you', she said. 'Would you like to use my cell phone to call someone'? Unfortunately, I had not brought Sachiko's cell phone number because I did not anticipate that there would be any problems. I told her I did not have any numbers to call and she left us, reluctantly, because she was still worried about us.

There was a place on the side of the hotel where cars could park. I took a quick look there but all I saw was a white BMW, another car with its bonnet up and a black Mercedes, so I returned to the front of the hotel. Then I remembered that one of Sachiko's colleagues, Robert, had called and left his cell phone number. I went into the hotel, had them call Robert, who then called Sachiko. It turned out she was waiting in her white BMW for me in the lot I had looked at and was getting a bit anxious herself. Robert called her and she came into the lobby and found me.

Sachiko drove us to Kinki University and after we had rested for a while, I gave my lecture – to around 200 students. When I corresponded with him about the lecture, Goh suggested that I use *Peanuts* comics, so I made a PowerPoint presentation with a number of *Peanuts* strips, plus some *Li'l Abner*, *Krazy Kat* and other comics and cartoons. I would speak for a few minutes and then Sachiko or Goh or both of them would discuss what I had said in Japanese. It struck me that the students did not find any of the comic strips or cartoons I showed them amusing, but I laboured on.

After my lecture, around 24 students remained to take part in my workshop. I had prepared a list of commonly used techniques of humour and some examples of humour and I wanted to have the students, in teams of three, figure out which techniques were working in the examples of humour. Sachiko and Goh were worried that the students would not 'get' my jokes so they added five of their own that were examples of Japanese humour. They got the first American joke, which was based on stereotypes, right away. After that we had trouble, so I went to the Japanese jokes. They were able to analyse some of them tolerably well, and seemed to be having a good time trying to figure out what makes the jokes and cartoons funny. Goh and Sachiko worked valiantly all afternoon trying to explain why some of the *Peanuts* strips were funny or amusing.

Poster for humour lecture

The lecture and workshop took three hours, but they seemed to pass in an instant. One of the professors in Sachiko's department had made a wonderful poster for the event and they gave me some of them to take back to the United States. Goh had to leave right after my lecture but Sachiko and most of her colleagues in the department she chairs took us to a Japanese restaurant, where we had one of the most wonderful meals I have ever had. It must have had eight or nine courses, each one beautifully presented and delicious. We were all drinking beer and as the evening progressed and we drank more beer, people were in very high spirits. So there was a lot of laughter that evening. The stereotype that the Japanese have no sense of humour is incorrect. When you spend time with Japanese people, you see that they love to laugh and have an excellent sense of humour. The dinner lasted three hours, so by the time Sachiko drove us to the train station in Osaka and we got back to Kyoto, it was close to midnight.

Visits to Himeji and Nara

In the remaining days we went to visit the castle in Himeji, which is generally considered to be the most important castle in Japan. We went on a Sunday and, to our surprise, there was a big festival in Himeji, and hundreds of police everywhere, handling traffic and the crowds. By chance, I got to see two festivals in Japan – although the festival in Himeji was not as large as the one in Asakusa. But there were mobs of people watching the events and people were carrying large banners and there was music and a woman on a loud speaker cheering everyone on.

Himeji castle

Japanese men waiting to participate in Himeji festival

Himeji festival seen from top of the Himeji castle

The train station in Himeji is over a wonderful shopping complex and food court and we found a little restaurant that had delicious gyoza – Japanese pot stickers. I had a bowl of soup and noodles and my wife had gyoza. We had thought of taking a bus to the castle but because of the festival there was no bus service there. But we did not need a bus because the castle is only a 15-minute walk from the station. The castle at Himeji is spectacular, and after you climb up endless flights of stairs you have a magnificent view of the whole area. Building that castle was a remarkable engineering feat.

Our last adventure was a trip to Nara. We took a train to Nara and then a bus for another hour to see some temple that I found rather uninteresting. We took a bus to the train station near the temple and after a short train ride we were in Nara again. We walked to the Todai-ji temple that had a gigantic Buddha in it. There were hundreds and hundreds of small deer around and people purchased cookies for them for 150 yen and fed them the cookies. Some of the deer learned to bob their head up and down to get more cookies.

Deer at Nara temple

The deer were very docile and you could pet them. A number of school children purchased toy antlers that they wore, which they found most amusing. After our visit to that temple, we wandered back to the train station and returned to Kyoto, our sightseeing adventures had come to an end. We spent our last day doing a bit of shopping and taking it easy and then we purchased tickets from Kyoto to the Kansai airport for 1860 yen, took a train to the airport and returned to the United States.

The United States and Japan: A Study in Polarities

In my journal I spent some time speculating about the differences between the United States and Japan. I had come to Japan to do research on Japanese culture and to see what I could discover about the country as a tourist but also as an observer. Until I stepped into a *Pachinko* parlour, I had not realized how noisy they were and how this noise assaulted ones senses. Some of these *Pachinko* parlours are enormous buildings and not little hole-in-the-wall places. And though I had eaten in Japanese restaurants in the United States a number of times, the meal I had in Osaka had some dishes – like parts of young lamprey eels – that were unlike anything I had ever eaten before.

The two countries have some things in common – baseball, McDonald's (and other American fast-food emporia), and raging consumer cultures, but they are different in any number of profound ways. The chart that follows offers a list of these differences. It is simplistic in some regards and perhaps forced here and there, but it still manages to throw each country into relief.

The United States	*Japan*
No feudalism	Feudal past
A former colony	Never a colony
Old democracy	Young democracy
New country	Old country
Large area	Small area
Continent	Islands
Egalitarian	Hierarchical
Food cheap	Food expensive
Multi-ethnic, multi-racial	Uni-ethnic, uni-racial
School children wear anything	School children in uniforms
Population growing	Population shrinking
Wheat	Rice
Beef	Fish

Christian	Buddhist/Shinto
President	Prime Minister
Republic	Monarchy
Violence ridden	Peaceful
Low suicide rate	High suicide rate
Children leave home ASAP	Parasite children stay at home until 30 or 40
'Fill it up' aesthetic	Emptiness aesthetic
Shake hands	Bow

You can see, from this list, that there are profound differences between American and Japanese culture – in everything from religion, ethnicity and their aesthetic sensibilities to the kind of foods they prefer. That may explain why Japan is so interesting a place to visit for Americans and people from other cultures as well, for Japan has a highly distinctive culture and one that enables people from other countries to see themselves in relief, as they compare their countries with Japan. One reason we travel, aside from the pleasure of seeing new places, is to learn more about ourselves. In this respect, Japan – with its refined aesthetic sensibility, with its sublime gardens, with its remarkable temples, with its vibrant popular culture and with its tradition of courtesy and kindness towards strangers – has a great deal to teach all of us.

References

Anon (1989) *Experiencing Japanese Culture: An Activity and Q-A Approach*. Tokyo: KEK Editorial Group.

Bakhtin, M. (1984) *Rabelais and His World*. Bloomington, IN: Indiana University Press.

Barthes, R. (1982) *Empire of Signs*. New York: Hill and Wang.

Barnouw, V. (1973) *Culture and Personality*. Homewood, IL: Dorsey.

Beardsley, R.K. (1965) *Twelve Doors to Japan*. New York: McGraw-Hill.

Berger, A.A. (ed.) (1974) *About Man: An Introduction to Anthropology*. Dayton, OH: Pflaum/Standard.

Berger, A.A. (2004) *Deconstructing Travel: Cultural Perspectives on Tourism*. Walnut Creek, CA: AltaMira Press.

Bornoff, N. (2000) *The National Geographic Traveler Japan*. Washington, DC: National Geographic Society.

Botton, A. de (2002) *The Art of Travel*. New York: Pantheon Books.

Carey, P. (2006) *Wrong about Japan*. New York: Vintage Books.

Caudill, W. and Plath, D.W. (1966) Who sleeps by whom? Parent–child involvement in urban Japanese families. *Psychiatry* 29, 344–366.

Chamberlain, B.H. (1905/2007) *Things Japanese: Being Notes on Various Subjects Connected with Japan*. Berkeley, CA: Stonebridge Press.

Cohen, E. (2008) The changing face of contemporary tourism. *Society* (July/August), 330–333.

Davidson, C.N. (1994) *36 Views of Mount Fuji*. New York: Plume Books.

Dichter, E. (2002) *The Strategy of Desire*. New Brunswick, NJ: Transaction.

Feiler, B.S. (1991) *Learning to Bow: Inside the Heart of Japan*. New York: Ticknor & Fields.

Freud, S. (1963) Character and anal eroticism. In P. Rieff (ed.) *Freud: Character and Culture*. New York: Collier Books.

Gorer, G. (1943) Themes in Japanese Culture. *Transactions of the New York Academy of Sciences* (Series II, Vol. V, pp. 106–124).

Gottdiener, M. (1995) *Postmodern Semiotics: Material Culture and the Form of Postmodern Life*. Cambridge, MA: Blackwell.

Gunther, J. (1938) *Inside Asia*. New York: Harper & Row.

Hall, I. (1998) *Cartels of the Mind: Japan's Intellectual Closed Shop*. New York: W.W. Norton.

Hall, S. (ed.) (1997) *Representation: Cultural Representation and Signifying Practices*. London: Sage.

Hearn, L. (1967) *A Japanese Miscellany*. Rutland, VT: Charles E. Tuttle.

Hyde, L. (1979) *The Gift: Imagination and the Erotic Life of Property*. New York: Vintage Books.

Ito, M. (2002) E-mail quoted in Howard Rheingold. *Smart Mobs: The Next Social Revolution*. New York: Perseus Books.

Ito, K. (2004) Growing up Japanese reading manga. *International Journal of Comic Art* 6 (2), 392–403.

Iyer, P. (1991) *The Lady and the Monk: Four Seasons in Kyoto*. New York: Knopf.

Johnson, S. (1974) The Christmas Gift Horse. In A.A. Berger (ed.) *About Man*. Dayton, OH: Pflaum.

Kerr, A. (1996) *Lost Japan*. Melbourne: Lonely Planet.

Kubey, R.W. (1996) Television dependence, diagnosis, and prevention: With commentary on video games, pornography, and media education. In T.M. MacBeth (ed.) *Tuning in to Young Viewers: Social Science Perspectives* (pp. 221–260). Thousand Oaks, CA: Sage.

La Barre, W. (1945) Some observations on character structure in the orient: The Japanese. *Psychiatry* 8, 319–412.

Latham, R.S. (1966) The artifact as cultural cipher. In L.B. Holland (ed.) *Who Designs America* (pp. 257–280). New York: Anchor Books.

Lebra, T.S. and Lebra, W.P. (eds) (1986) *Japanese Culture and Behavior: Selected Readings* (revised edn). Honolulu: University of Hawaii Press.

Lévi-Strauss, C. (1970) *Tristes Tropiques*. New York: Athaneum.

Loveday, L. and Chiba, S. (1986) Aspects of the development towards a visual culture in respect of comics: Japan. In A. Silbermann and H.D. Dryoff (eds) *Comics and Visual Culture* (pp. 158–184). Munich, Germany: K.G. Saur Verlag.

Lyotard, J-F. (1984) *The Postmodern Condition: A Report on Knowledge*. Minneapolis: University of Minnesota Press.

MacCannell, D. (1976) *The Tourist: A New Theory of the Leisure Class*. New York: Schocken.

Malinowski, B. (1921/1961) *Argonauts of the Western Pacific*. New York: E.P. Dutton.

Martinez, D.P. (ed.) (1998) *The World of Japanese Popular Culture*. Cambridge: Cambridge University Press.

Masaru Tamamoto (2009) Japan's crisis of the mind. *The New York Times*, 2 March, p. A21.

McQueen, I. (1997) *A Budget Travel Guide: Japan*. Tokyo: Kodansha International.

Milgram, S. (1976) The image freezing machine. *Society* (November/December), Vol. 14, 7–12.

Morton, D. and Tsunoi, N. (1989) *The Best of Tokyo*. Rutland, VT: Charles E. Tuttle.

Mosher, G. (1980) *Kyoto: A Contemplative Guide*. Rutland, VT: Charles E. Tuttle.

Mura, D. (1991) *Turning Japanese: Memoirs of a Sansei*. New York: Atlantic Monthly Press.

Onishi, N. (2004) Japan and China: National character writ large. *The New York Times*, 17 March.

Phillips, C. (2005) *Time Out Tokyo*. London: Time Out Guides.

Rapaille, C. (2006) *The Culture Code: An Ingenious Way to Understand Why People Around the World Live and Buy as They Do*. New York: Broadway Books.

Reiber, B. and Spencer, J. (2004) *Frommer's Japan* (7th edn). New York: Wiley Publishing Inc.

Reischauer, E.O. (1977) _The Japanese_. Cambridge, MA: Harvard University Press.
Reischauer, E.O. and Jansen, M.B. (1994) _The Japanese Today: Change and Continuity_ (enlarged edn). Cambridge, MA: Harvard University Press.
Rheingold, H. (2003) _Smart Mobs: The Next Social Revolution_. New York: Perseus Books.
Richie, D. and Lowitz, L. (2005) _The Japanese Journals_. Albany, CA: Stonebridge.
Richmond, S. and Dodd, J. (2005) _The Rough Guide to Japan_ (3rd edn). New York: Rough Guides.
Saussure, F. de (1966) _Course in General Linguistics_. New York: McGraw-Hill.
Sebeok, T. (1977) _A Perfusion of Signs_. Bloomington, IN: Indiana University Press.
Seidensticker, E. (1991) _Tokyo Rising: The City Since the Great Earthquake_. Cambridge, MA: Harvard University Press.
Simmel, G. (1997). The adventure. In D. Frisby and M. Featherstone (eds) _Simmel on Culture_. London: Sage.
Smith, P. (1997) _Japan: A Reinterpretation_. New York: Pantheon Books.
Solomon, M., Bamossy, G. and Askegard, S. (2002) _Consumer Behavior: A European Perspective_. Upper Saddle River, NJ: Prentice-Hall.
Sterngold, J. (1991) New Japanese lesson: Running a 7–11. _The New York Times_, 9 May.
Takada, N. and Lampkin, R.L. (1997) _The Japanese Way: Aspects of Behavior, Attitudes, and Customs of the Japanese_. New York: Passport Books.
Thiro, R. (ed.) (2000) _DK Eyewitness Travel Guides: Japan_. London: Dorling Kindersley.
Treib, M. and Herman, H. (1993) _A Guide to the Gardens of Kyoto_. Tokyo: Shufunotomo.
Wang, N. (2000) _Tourism and Modernity: A Sociological Analysis_. Oxford: Pergamon.
Warner, L. (1952) _The Enduring Art of Japan_. Cambridge, MA: Harvard University Press.
Wolf, S. (ed.) (1998) _Fodor's Japan_. New York: Fodor's Travel Publications.
Yamashita, S. (2003) _Bali and Beyond: Explorations in the Anthropology of Tourism_. New York: Berghahn Books.

Index

7-Eleven convenience stores
– history of, 98-99
– similarity to vending machines, 99
– statistics about, 98
100 Yen stores
– Daiso chain in Japan, 108
– usefulness for tourists, 109

Abe, Goh, xi, 144-146
"Adventure", 123
American occupation of Japan, 129-130
"Artifact as Cultural Cipher", 93
Art of Travel, 12
Askegard, Soren, 103
"Aspects of the Development Towards a
    Visual Culture in Respect of Comics:
    Japan", 86

Bakhtin, Mikhail, 82-83
Bali, 42-43
Bali and Beyond, 42
Bamossy, Gary, 103
Barnouw, Victor, 19
Barre, Weston La, 17, 19, 115
Barthes, Roland, xx, 51, 53-55, 114-115, 116-
    117
Baseball
– Japanese fans, 78
– Japanese way of playing, 77-78
Baudrillard, Jean, 120
Beardsley, Richard K., 17
Benedict, Ruth, 18
Bento boxes
– Japanese aesthetic reflected in, 118-119
– variety of food in, 118
Boorstin, Daniel, 84
Bornoff, N., 14
Botton, Alain de, 11, 32

Carey, Peter, 90
*Cartels of the Mind: Japan's Intellectual Closed
    Shop*, 61
Caudill, William, 18
Chamberlain, Basil Hall, xv, xvi, xviii, 67

"Character and Anal Eroticism", 18
Chiba, Naomi, xi, 26
Chiba, Satomi, 86-87
Coda
– first encounters with helpful Japanese
    persons, 132-133
– food courts in department stores, 140-141
– Himeji and Nara visits, 147-149
– Japanese supermarkets, 142
– Kanazawa, 139—140
– Kyoto, 142-144, 146
– long distance bus travel's pleasures,
    136-137
– lost in the Shimbashi subway station, 135
– Sanja Matsuri Festival 133
– Takayama adventures, 137-139
– teaching Japanese students about
    American humor, 144-146
– USA and Japan polarities, 150-151
Cohen, Erik, 84, 85, 129, 130
Comics and Visual Culture, 87
*Commercialized Crafts of Thailand Hill Tribes
    and Lowland Villages*, 129
Consumer Behavior: A European Perspective,
    103
Consumer Society: Myths and Structures,
    120
Copenhagen, 41
Core Sociological Dichotomies, 122
Course in General Linguistics, 54
Cronin, Michael, 130
*Cultural Representations and Signifying
    Practices* 121
Culture and Personality, 19

Davidson, Cathy N., xi
*Deconstructing Travel: Cultural Perspectives
    on Tourism*, 6
Department stores
– customer is king, 110
– decline in sales in, 110
– high cost of goods in, 110-111
– importance of food halls in, 109
– similarities with temples, 111-113

Dichter, Ernest, 93
DK Eyewitness Travel Guide, 15
Dodd, Jan, 14, 15
Durkheim, Emile, 122-123

educational system
– bullying in, 73-74
– education mothers, 74
– escalator system, 72-73
– examination hell, 73
– stress caused by, 72-74
– suicide, 73
Elements of Semiology, 51
Empire of Signs, xviii, xx, 53, 114
Enduring Art of Japan, 79
exotic and erotic
– Greek root of word "exotic", 65
– Japanese culture as, 66-67
– tourists search for, 65

Feiler, Bruce S., xi, 71, 73, 74
Flinn, John, 31
Fodor's *Exploring Japan*, 57-58
Freud, Sigmund, 18
fugu
– Barthes on rawness in Japanese food, 116-117
– cost of blue finned tuna, 116
– fish madness in Japan, 116
– risking life to eat fish, 117

geishas
– and touristic "time travel", 68
– as sex workers, 62
– compared to salarymen, 67-69
– decline in number of, 62
– decline of, 64-65
– fantasies about Japan and, 61-62
– the exotic and the erotic, 65-67
– training of, 63
gift giving
– cultural importance of, 103
– economic impact of, 107
– functions of, 107
– functions of in Japanese society, 103-104
– importance of the package, 103
– in United States, 104-105
– Melanesian Kula and, 106-107
– rules for Japan, 105-106
Gift: Imagination and the Erotic Life of Property, 104
Google, 45, 47
Gorer, Geoffrey, 17, 18
Guide to the Gardens of Kyoto, 34, 80

Gunther, John, 21-23

Hakone, 26
Hall, I., 61
Hall, Stuart, 121
Hearn, Lafcadio, 51
Herman, H., 34
Herman, Ron, 80-81
high tech toilets
– Japanese cultural anxiety about dirt, 95
– Japanese perfectionism and, 95, 95-96
– loathing of faeces in Japan, 95
– part of material culture, 93
– Toto Washlet, 94
hikikomori, 23
– as Japan's "lost generation", 72
– educational system and, 72-74
– Japanese conformist culture and, 75
– Japanese family life and, 74-75
– number of in Japan, 72
– psychological illness hypothesis, 75-76
– resistance to a destructive culture, 75-76
– school uniforms and, 71-72
– violence in Japanese schools, 73-74
Himeji, 27
Hiroshima, 25, 27, 30
Hyde, Lewis, 104

Ikiru, 102
"Image Freezing Machine", 12
Imber, Jonathan, 120
Inside Asia, 21
Inside Europe, 21
Internet sites on Japan
– Japan Tourism on Google, 46-47
– Frommer's Travel Talk on Japan, 48-49
– Googling Japan, 44
Irish Tourism, 130
Ito, Kinko, 85-86
Ito Mizuko, 56-57
Iyer, Pico, 1, 10, 17

Jansen, Marius B., xi, 89, 125, 128
Japan
– American fast food franchises in, 117
– as conformist culture, 75-76
– cost of visiting, xvii
– David Mura on, 1
– decline of geishas, 23
– decline of salarymen, 23
– Emperor worship, 1
– family income and expenditures,
– food courts in department stores, 140-141
– geography of, 3

– gift giving, 103-107
– guidebook perspectives on, 13-17
– hyper-modernism and postmodernism, xviii
– imagined, real, and remembered, 10-13
– Japanese National Tourist Organization (JNTO), xix, 36, 45
– long distance bus travel in, 136-137
– modernization, 66
– national character, 17-24
– on the Internet, 45-49
– *Pachinko*, xviii, 99-103
– Pico Iyer on, 1
– popular culture, xvii
– postmodernism and, 128-129
– postmodernism in, 91-92
– purity in, 95-96
– railway stations, xviii
– safe to visit, xvii
– statistics about, 3-4
– stereotypes in John Gunther's books, 21
– suggested itinerary of, 26-28
– Tokyo subway system, 112-115
– tourism, xviii
– tourism and cultural change, 121-130
– tourists desire for erotic, 66-67
– tours of, 24-25
– traditional culture, xvii
Japan: A Budget Travel Guide, 15
"Japan and China: National Character Writ Large", 19
Japan: A Reinterpretation, 60
Japanese Culture and Behavior: Selected Readings 23
Japanese flag
– description of, 69-70
– nationalism and, 71
– symbolic significance of, 70-71
Japanese national character
– and toilet training of children, 17
– homogeneity of population, 17
– John Gunther's stereotypes of, 22-23
– neatness and ritualistic cleanliness, 17
– prejudice against immigration, 20
– preoccupation with tidiness, ritual and orderliness, 17
– role of isolation in forming, 17
– secretiveness, hiding of emotions and attitudes, 17
– sleeping arrangements in families, 18
Japanese National Tourist Organization (JNTO), xix, 28, 36
Japanese Today: Change and Continuity, 89, 125-126

Japanese Today, 89
Japan Journals, 57
"Japan's Crisis of the Mind", 19-20
Journal of Tourism and Cultural Change, 122

Kamakura, 26
Kanai, Gen, 34
Kanazawa, 24, 139-140
Katzenstein, Gary, xi
Kerr, Alex, xi, 101, 102, 102-103
Kinki University, 144-145
Kitazume, Sachiko, xi, 144, 145-146
Kiyoshi, Kanzaki, 63
Krazy Kat, 145
Kubey, Robert W., 100-101
Kurosawa, Akira, xxi, 102
Kyoto, 12, 25, 27, 142-143
– bus trip to Kyoto, 142-144
– free tour guides, 49
– historical gardens of Kyoto, 81
– shrines and temples, 27
– sight seeing in Kyoto, 143-144
– time spent in Kyoto, 136
Kyoto University, 72
Kyoto: A Contemplative Guide, 79-80

Lathan, Richard S., 93
Learning to Bow, 73
Lebra, Takie Sugiyama, xi, 23
Lebra, William P., xi, 23
Lévi-Strauss, Claude, xix, xx, 127
Libra, William P., 234
Li'l Abner, 145
Lost Japan, 101
Loveday, Lee, 86-87
Lowie, Robert H., xix
Lyotard, Jean-François, 91-92

MacCannell, Dean, xxi
Malinowski, Bronislaw, 106-107
manga
– erotic appeals in, 87-88
– growth of, 87-88
– role in Japanese culture, 89-90
– role in Japanese learning to read, 86
– socializing aspects of, 86
– statistics about, 87
– typical contents of, 86
Martinez, D.P., 131
Marx, Karl, 122
Mauss, Marcel, 104
McQueen, Ian, 15, 16
Milgram, Stanley, 12
Mosher, Gouverneur, 78-79

Moynihan, Daniel Patrick, 121
Mura, David, 1

National Geographic Traveler Japan, 13
"New Japanese Lesson: Running a 7-11",
99
New York Times, 99
Nikko, 26
Norma, Caroline, 63-64

O'Connor, Barbara, 130
Office of Travel and Tourism Industries
(OTTI), 39
Onishi, Norimitsu, 19
Osaka, 144-147
otaku
– definition of, 76, 90
– description of, 90

Pachinko
– as form of gambling, 96
– economic impact of, 101
– homogenous Japanese society and,
102-103
– immersion aspects of, 100-101
– influence of Pachinko aesthetic, 101-102
– Japanese temperament and, 102-103
– number of parlours in Japan, 99
Palace Side Hotel, 142-143
Peirce, Charles Sanders, 53, 55
Phipps, Alison, xi
Plath, David W., 18
Postmodern Condition: A Report of Knowledge,
92
Primitive Society, xix

Rapaille, Clotaire
– lack of space in Japan, 95
– reasons for Japanese perfectionism, 95
Rashomon, xxi
Reischauer, Edwin O., xi, 89
Rheingold, Howard, 56-57
Richie, Donald, xi, 57
Richmond, Simon, 14, 15
Rieff, Philip, 18
Rikidozan, 58
Robinson, Michael D., xi
rock gardens
– as icons of Japanese culture, 79
– characteristics of, 79-81
– not popular with Japanese public, 81
– symbolism in, 80-81
– traditional Japanese culture and, 81
Rough Guide to Japan, 14

salaryman
– contrasted with geishas, 68-69
– decline of, 68-69
San Francisco Chronicle, 31
Sanja Matsuri Festival
– authenticity and, 84-85
– carnivalesque quality of, 82-83
– description of, 81-83
– popularity of, 81
– postmodern theory and, 84-85
– role of *Mikashi* in, 81-82
Saussure, Ferdinand de, 30, 54, 65
Scott, David, 60, 71
Sebeok, T., 55
Seidensticker, Edwin, xi, 64, 65, 77, 129
semiotic theory
– basic notions in, 53-56
– codes, 56-57
– semiology, 53
– semiotics, 53
– Roland Barthes on Japanese culture, 53
– signs, signifiers, signifieds, 54-56
shinjinrui
– definition of, 90-91
– role in Japanese society, 90-91
Simmel, Georg, 32, 120, 123
Smith, Patrick, xi, 51, 60
Society magazine, 12
Solomon, Michael, 103
"Some Observations on Character Structure
in the Orient: The Japanese", 17
Star Man, 1
Strategy of Desire, 93
sumo wrestlers
– as iconic figures, 57-58
– description of matches, 58-59
– long history in Japan, 58
– psychoanalytic perspective on, 60-61

Tamamoto, Masaru, 20
Takayama, 24, 27, 136-139
"Television Dependence, Diagnosis, and
Prevention: With Commentary on Video
Games, Pornography, and Media
Education", 100-101
"The Image Freezing Machine', 12
"Themes in Japanese Culture", 17
Things Japanese, 67
Thiro, R., 15
Toennies, F., 122-123
Tokyo
– Asakusa Senzoku hotel, 132
– Barthes on empty center of, 114
– efficiency of subway, 115

– Sanja Matsuri Festival, 133
– Shimbashi subway station, 135
– sites of touristic importance, 26
– size of, 112
– size of central city area, 114
– subway lines, 112
– subway map, 114
– Tsukiji fish market, 116
– Ueno, 136
Tokyo Rising: The City Since the Great Earthquake, 64, 77
Tokyo subway
– helpfulness of subway riders, 115
– lines found in, 112-113
– map of, 114
– size of Tokyo and, 114-115
Tonkiss, Fran, 122
tourism
– activities of American tourists in Japan, 48
– as form of consumption, 125
– characteristics of, 6
– cultural change and, xxi
– definitions of, 5-6
– impact on politics, 126
– Japanese tourists in foreign countries, 41-42
– largest industry in world, xxi
– role in social change, xxi
– statistics on world tourism, 36-39
– use of semiotic analysis, xxi
– tourism and cultural change in Japan
– classical theories of social change, 122-124
– kinds of tourists and cultural change, 124-125
– kinds of tourists and their impact, 124-125
– sources of cultural change, 125-129
Tourism and Modernity, 127
tourism (kinds of) in Japan
– adventure, 8
– cultural, 7-8

– disaster, 9-10
– ecotourism, 8
– food, 8
– sex, 8-9
– sports, 9
– uses and gratifications, 29-32
Tourist: A New Theory of the Leisure Class, xxi, 85
Toyoko Inn, xvii
Treib, Mark, 34, 80-81
Tristes Tropiques, xix, 127
Tsukamoto, Yasutake, xi
Twelve Doors to Japan, 17

USA Today, 87
uses and gratifications of tourism
– experience the beautiful, 29
– help reinforce national identity, 30
– obtain a sense of community with others, 31
– participate in history, 29
– renew oneself, 31-33
– satisfy our curiosity, 29
– to be amused and entertained, 29

vending machines
– number of in Japan, 96
– products sold in, 97
– psychoanalytic functions of, 97-98
– symbolic significance of, 96

Wang, Ning, 127-128
Warner, Langdon, 78
Watanabe, Mariko, xi, xvi
Weber, Max, 122, 122-123, 123
"Who Sleeps by Whom? Parent-Child Involvement in Urban Japanese Families", 18

Yamashita, Shinji, 42, 126
Youth Tourism in Israel, 130